# French Artists in Rome:
## Ingres to Degas, 1803–1873

Curated by Olivier Bonfait and Roger Diederen

Edited by Roger Diederen

Essay by Olivier Bonfait and Antoinette Le Normand-Romain

## Dahesh Museum of Art

New York 2003

# TABLE OF CONTENTS

This catalogue accompanies an exhibition on view
from September 3 to November 2, 2003 at

DAHESH MUSEUM OF ART

580 Madison Avenue
New York, NY 10022
www.daheshmuseum.org

Front cover: HIPPOLYTE FLANDRIN, *Figure Study:
Polites, Son of Priam, Observing the Movements of the
Greeks towards Troy*, 1834 (detail, repr. p. 27)

Back cover: JEAN AUGUSTE DOMINIQUE INGRES,
*François-Marius Granet*, 1807–1809 (repr. p. 18)

© 2003 Dahesh Museum of Art
ISBN NO. 0-9654793-0-7
Library of Congress Control No. 2003110315

Design: Lawrence Sunden, Inc.
Printing: Randem Printing Co.

## DIRECTOR'S FOREWORD

It has been both an honor and a pleasure to become Director of the Dahesh Museum of Art as it opens a magnificent new home at 580 Madison Avenue in midtown Manhattan *and* brings to New York so extraordinary an exhibition as *French Artists in Rome: Ingres to Degas, 1803-1873.* The aesthetic quality and historical significance of the works of art in this groundbreaking exhibition are exceptional, and we are deeply grateful to Curator Olivier Bonfait, Director Richard Peduzzi, and their colleagues at the Académie de France à Rome for organizing this project and then sharing it with us.

Since it opened to the public in 1995, the Dahesh Museum of Art has been devoted to collecting, exhibiting, and interpreting 19th- and early 20th-century academic art. The fact that *French Artists in Rome* is being presented only in Rome and New York demonstrates how the Dahesh has succeeded in fulfilling its unique mission and enhancing New York's cultural vitality in the short space of eight years. I salute the energy and intelligence brought to the coordination of this project by the Dahesh's own Curator, Roger Diederen, and I would like to extend my gratitude to all of our colleagues here for their efforts to make the project a reality on a very tight schedule.

*French Artists in Rome* would not be possible at all, however, without the generous loans approved by a broad range of institutions and private collectors worldwide. I thank all of them for agreeing to live without their treasures for a few more months, and hope that each will find an opportunity to see how well these artworks look in the heart of Manhattan this autumn.

Finally, the Board of Trustees deserve a thunderous round of applause for their vision of a larger and more welcoming Dahesh Museum of Art—a vision that has finally been achieved this year at 580 Madison Avenue. I congratulate all of them, and especially Amira Zahid, for their generosity and determination to see the expansion through. We are all proud to open this splendid new home for academic art with *French Artists in Rome,* an exhibition about one of the most influential academies of all.

Peter Trippi
Director
Dahesh Museum of Art

**NYSCA**
New York State Council on the Arts

Made possible in part with public funds from the New York State Council on the Arts, a State agency

## Acknowledgments

First and foremost, I wish to thank Olivier Bonfait for being immediately enthusiastic about the idea of presenting his exhibition at the Dahesh Museum of Art. He and the staff at the Académie de France à Rome—Marie-Christine Labourdette, Angela Stahl, Anne-Lise Desmas, Nathalie Motte, and Florence Hérubel—were most hospitable during my stay in Rome and extremely helpful in the realization of bringing this ambitious project to New York.

At the Dahesh Museum of Art, I thank Director Peter Trippi, Associate Director Michael Fahlund, and my curatorial colleagues Stephen Edidin, Lisa Small and Frank Verpoorten for their support and collegiality. Every other staff member has also contributed tremendously to this complex undertaking, all the while setting a new standard for exhibitions at the Dahesh Museum of Art.

Furthermore, I would like to thank all institutional and private lenders, as well as the many friends and colleagues who were so generous in providing support and sharing their knowledge: Claude Allemand-Cosneau, Louise d'Argencourt, Carlos Eduardo Araujo, Jacques Beauffet, Sylvain Bellenger, Christine Besson, Max Blumberg, Laura Bennett, Mark Brady, Curtis L. Carter, Cécile Contassot, Denis Coutagne, Brigitte Maurice-Chabard, Françoise Cohen, Michael Conforti, Philip Conisbee, Henri-Claude Cousseau, Martine Dancer, Anne Dary, Nanne Dekking, Emmanuelle Delapierre, Corinne Diserens, Guy Faucher, Marie-Cécile Forest, Jean-René Gaborit, Jay Gates, Bertrand Gautier, Stéphane Guégan, Anne d'Harnoncourt, Annette Haudiquet, Colta B. Ives, William Johnston, Michel Hilaire, Annie Jacques, Charles Janoray, Eik Kahng, Mehdi Korchane, Philippe Le Leyzour, Antoinette Le Normand-Romain, Isabelle Leroy-Jay Lemaistre, Serge Lemoine, Christophe Leribault, Henri Loyrette, Marie-Noëlle Maynard, Philippe de Montebello, Mr. and Mrs. Lee Munder, Annick Notter, Patrick Le Nouëne, Richard Peduzzi, Matthieu Pinette, Anne Pingeot, Earl A. Powell III, Patrick Ramade, Richard Rand, Katharine Lee Reid, Céline Rincé-Vaslin, Joseph Rishel, Chantal Rouquet, Nathalie Roux, Didier Rykner, Marie-Catherine Sahut, Laurent Salomé, Alan Salz, Emmanuel Schwartz, Marcia Steele, Stanton Thomas, Gary Tinterow, Jennifer Vanim, Florence Viguier, Georges Vigne, Gary Vikan, and those who wish to remain anonymous. Marc Vincent and Henry Krawitz have expertly translated and edited the essay by Olivier Bonfait and Antoinette Le Normand-Romain, and I thank these authors for sharing their text. It was also a great pleasure to work with Dan Kershaw who designed the exhibition.

Ultimately, however, this exhibition and the wonderful new facility that houses it would not have been possible without the unflagging support and generosity of the Museum's Board of Trustees, to whom this exhibition is dedicated.

Roger Diederen
Curator

## Lenders to the Exhibition

*France*
Aix-en-Provence, Musée Granet
Amiens, Musée de Picardie
Angers, Galerie David d'Angers
Angers, Musée des Beaux-Arts
Arras, Musée des Beaux-Arts
Autun, Musée Rolin
Carcassonne, Musée des Beaux-Arts
Clermont-Ferrand, Musée d'art Roger-Quillot
Gray, Musée Baron Martin
Le Havre, Musée Malraux
Lons-le-Saunier, Musée des Beaux-Arts
Montauban, Musée Ingres
Montpellier, Musée Fabre
Nantes, Musée des Beaux-Arts
Nîmes, Musée des Beaux-Arts
Orléans, Musée des Beaux-Arts
Paris, École Nationale Supérieure des Beaux-Arts
Paris, Musée Gustave Moreau
Paris, Musée du Louvre
Paris, Musée d'Orsay
Rouen, Musée des Beaux-Arts
Saint-Étienne, Musée d'Art moderne
Tours, Musée des Beaux-Arts
Troyes, Musée des Beaux-Arts
Valenciennes, Musée des Beaux-Arts
Anonymous Collectors

*Italy*
Académie de France à Rome
Anonymous Collectors

*United States*
Baltimore, The Walters Art Museum
Cleveland Museum of Art
Cornish, NH, Max Blumberg and Carlos Eduardo Araujo
Milwaukee, Haggerty Museum of Art, Marquette University
New York, Didier Aaron, Inc.
New York, Charles Janoray Gallery
New York, The Metropolitan Museum of Art
Palm Beach, Mr. and Mrs. Lee Munder
Washington DC, National Gallery of Art
Washington DC, The Phillips Collection
Williamstown, Sterling and Francine Clark Art Institute
Anonymous Collectors

# INTRODUCTION

Rome, the central repository of Western civilization, is also the home of numerous foreign academies founded to give young artists the opportunity to learn from the city's great cultural treasures. The oldest, the Académie de France à Rome, was established by King Louis XIV in 1666 and moved to its present home, the Villa Medici, in 1803. Commemorating the bicentennial of that relocation, Olivier Bonfait, curator of the academy, organized a major exhibition at the Villa Medici under the title: *D'Ingres à Degas. Les artistes français à Rome*. It analyzes the art created by French artists in Rome during the golden age of the Villa Medici, which lasted roughly from the beginning of Napoleon's Italian conquests through the country's unification in 1870.

To celebrate the opening of the new home of the Dahesh Museum of Art—an institution dedicated to reevaluating 19th-century European academic art—it seemed highly appropriate to show a major selection of paintings and sculptures from this extraordinary exhibition at the Villa Medici. The important rite of passage that countless French artists experienced by living and working in Rome is one of the key aspects that shaped academic art throughout the 19th century. After students at the École des Beaux-Arts in Paris won the prestigious *prix de Rome* competition, they were awarded a residency of up to five years at the Villa Medici, underwritten by the French government. This Roman sojourn was intended to immerse the artist in the great heritage of ancient and Renaissance masters and to nurture future generations who would sustain this revered tradition.

Rome had already inspired artists for centuries. It was traditionally a place of formation as well as a point of departure for many an artistic career. In order to better understand the French Academy's role within the artistic milieu of 19th-century France, the exhibition not only examines the unifying links between *pensionnaires* (the resident student artists) and directors at the Villa Medici, but also explores contacts with visiting artists such as Gustave Moreau and Edgar Degas, as well as with those who chose Rome as their primary residence. A communal spirit was fostered not only by the evening academy drawing sessions introduced by Jean Auguste Dominique Ingres, but also by excursions into the countryside in order to paint from nature. This exhibition further demonstrates how the French Academy, despite its strict regulations, allowed for great variety in artistic creation. The works on display show a stylistic evolution from Ingres's academicism of the 1830s through the eclecticism of the 1860s and beyond.

*D'Ingres à Degas. Les artistes français à Rome* was one of an extraordinary triad of Roman exhibitions organized in Spring 2003 under the unifying title *Maestà di Roma. Da Napoleone all'Unità d'Italia*. The other two exhibitions—conceived by the late Stefano Susinno and organized by the Galleria Nazionale d'Arte Moderna and its curator Sandra Pinto—featured a broad survey of 19th-century Roman work by European and American artists (*Universale ed Eterna* at the Scuderie del Quirinale) and a thematic examination of Roman art production in the 19th century (*Capitale delle Arti* at the Galleria Nazionale). The two monumental catalogues that resulted from this collaboration will remain the standard reference works on this subject for years to come.[1] The present book was conceived as an English language guide to the Dahesh Museum of Art's presentation of the Villa Medici exhibition. The New York exhibition and publication follow the concepts and outline formulated by Olivier Bonfait and his extensive team of scholars. While space constraints necessitated a reduction in scale of the Dahesh presentation, the extraordinary quality of this exhibition has been left undiminished. Even far from home, Rome's majesty continues to shine bright.

Roger Diederen
Curator

1. Olivier Bonfait, e.a. *Maestà di Roma. Da Napoleone all'Unità d'Italia—D'Ingres à Degas, Les artistes français à Rome*, exh. cat. Académie de France à Rome, Villa Médicis, March 7–June 29, 2003 (Milano, Electa, 2003), 616 pages, French and Italian edition. Stefano Susinno, Sandra Pinto, e.a., *Maestà di Roma. Da Napoleone all'Unità d'Italia—Universale ed Eterna—Capitale delle Arti*, one exhibition catalogue for two concurrent shows at the Galleria Nazionale d'Arte Moderna and the Scuderie del Quirinale, Rome, March 7–June 29, 2003 (Milano, Electa, 2003), 716 pages, Italian edition only.

# French Governmental Arts Organizations: An Overview

The *Académie royale de peinture et de sculpture*, founded under King Louis XIV in 1648, sought to elevate the position of the artist beyond that of a commercial craftsman. The institution was abolished during the French Revolution of 1789, and replaced by the *Institut de France* (often referred to as the *Institut*) in 1795. This supreme body oversaw the government's involvement with the arts and sciences and, to this day, still comprises the following five academies: *Académie française* [French Academy], *Académie des inscriptions et belles-lettres* [Academy of Inscriptions and Literature], *Académie des sciences* [Academy of Sciences], *Académie des beaux-arts* [Academy of Fine Arts], and *Académie des sciences morales et politiques* [Academy of Moral and Political Sciences].

The *Académie des beaux-arts*, founded in 1803 as a successor to the *Académie royale de peinture et de sculpture*, controlled the official exhibitions, called the *Salons* after the Salon Carré in the Louvre, where these exhibitions originated in the 17th century. The *Académie des beaux-arts* also oversaw the *École des beaux-arts* (now *École nationale supérieure des beaux-arts*), where the official art instruction took place, as well as its outpost in Rome, the *Académie de France à Rome*. The latter had been founded in 1666 at the urging of painter Charles Lebrun. Winners of the annual *prix de Rome* contest at the *École* in Paris were provided with a government stipend that allowed them to study classical and Renaissance art in Rome for a period of up to five years. To compete, an artist had to be of French nationality, male, under 30 years of age, and single. He had to have met the entrance requirements of the *École* and have the support of a well-known art teacher. The competition was grueling, involving several stages before the final one, in which ten competitors were sequestered in studios for 72 days to complete their final history paintings and sculptures. There were separate competitions for painters, sculptors, engravers, architects and composers.

With the artistic reforms of 1863, the *Académie des beaux-arts* lost much of its power: the *École* dissociated itself from the *Académie* and its curriculum was revised.

In 1871, however, the members of the *Académie* regained jurisdiction over the *prix de Rome* competition. While the *prix de Rome* was abolished in 1968, these institutions still exist today, but none have maintained the significance they held in France's cultural life during the first three quarters of the 19th century.

## Directors of the Académie de France à Rome (1803–1873)

Joseph-Benoît Suvée (1795–1806)

Guillaume Guillon Lethière (1807–1815)

Charles Thévenin (1816–1822)

Pierre-Narcisse Guérin (1823–1828)

Horace Vernet (1829–1834)

Jean Auguste Dominique Ingres (1835–1840)

Victor Schnetz (1841–1846)

Jean Alaux (1847–1852)

Victor Schnetz (1853–1865)

Joseph-Nicolas Robert-Fleury (1866)

Ernest Hébert (1867–1872)

Jules Lenepveu (1873–1878)

# L'École de Rome

Olivier Bonfait and Antoinette Le Normand-Romain

Mr. Chifflart is a Grand Prix de Rome winner and, miracle of miracles, he has originality. His stay in the Eternal City has not extinguished the strength of his intellect; which, after all, only proves one thing, namely, that only those who are too weak to live there perish, and that the *École* humiliates only those who are devoted to humility.

—Charles Baudelaire[1]

FOUNDED BY LOUIS XIV in 1666 and abolished on November 25, 1792, under pressure notably from Jacques-Louis David, and during a period when every institution of the ancien régime was being reexamined, the Académie de France à Rome [French Academy in Rome] was reestablished between 1795 and 1798 as the *École de Rome* [School of Rome]. This rebirth occurred in three stages: the reestablishment of the school and the naming of a director; the setting forth of regulations; and the move to the Villa Medici.

"The re-establishment of the École de France in Italy," wrote Guinguené, "is thus the greatest contribution that the government could make to the arts."[2] Despite efforts to place at its head François-André Vincent or Jean-Baptiste Regnault, it was Joseph-Benoît Suvée[3] who was named "director of the École de France in Italy" on October 23, 1795, by order of the Comité d'Instruction publique [Committee for Public Education]. The choice of Rome as the site of the school was quickly determined: "We have [there] a palazzo with all the conveniences, and all the antique models are virtually intact. Besides, Rome is a world unto itself for the arts, and Florence . . . has nothing compared to Rome. The painters who come to Italy to study spend six months in Florence, the same in Naples, and ten years in Rome, so vast are the resources of this city compared to the rest."[4]

Thanks to Suvée's perseverance and organizational skills, coupled with the reestablishment of French domination in Rome, the school's reorganization followed the reestablishment of the Prix de Rome in 1797 (decree of 23 Fructidor, Year VI, September 9, 1798).[5] The ruling of April 4, 1799, which restated some of Suvée's propositions that he had sent to the Ministry of the Interior on December 2, 1797, fixed the number and quality of the *pensionnaires* [resident student artists] (a total of 15,

evenly divided among the disciplines of painting, sculpture, and architecture),[6] set forth their obligations and specified the hours that a model could pose and the hours of study of antique statuary or of drapery folds on a mannequin. Every year the *pensionnaires* had to execute works, which were then publicly exhibited at the École in Rome and then sent to Paris to be submitted to the "judgment of the professors from the specialized schools devoted to painting, sculpture, and architecture." Starting in 1804, it was the Beaux-Arts class of the Institut de France that judged the *envois de Rome* [works of art sent to the Academy in Paris for review], thus reinforcing its hold over the *École de Rome*. The result of this examination was then transmitted to the director of the *École de Rome*, "who would inform each *pensionnaire* about what concerned him."[7] The Academy was conceived like a school, on the model of both the Napoleonic lycée and the Institut: the *pensionnaires* had to live at the school, eat their meals together at fixed times, obtain the permission of the director for any absences, and wear a uniform. Paid by the state, they came to Rome to further their studies and to become artists of the nation.

Where to situate this school? Even before his arrival in Rome in 1801, Suvée knew that to return it to the Palazzo Mancini on the Via del Corso—its location since 1725—would be difficult; the building had been ransacked several times between 1792 and 1798 and had proved itself ill suited to serve this function. If, like Pierre-René Cacault, Suvée had preferred that the *École* be installed in the Palazzo Farnese, he very quickly embraced the choice of the Villa Medici, which had been proposed as early as 1798 and approved over and above the opposition of the Church, which worried that "most of the painters, having the most corrupt opinions on matters of politics and religion, and being quite depraved [would be] in a place that dominated Rome in its entirety and included even a large portion of the city walls."[8] On May 18, 1803, the transfer from the Palazzo Mancini to the Villa Medici was officially ratified by the French Republic, led at that time by First Consul Napoleon Bonaparte, and the Kingdom of Etruria; this exchange, having transpired before a notary, could not be annulled in 1814. In December 1803 twelve *pensionnaires* arrived at the Villa Medici, whose refurbishment was not yet complete.

The results of the Prix de Rome competition were proclaimed in October during the annual public session of the Académie des Beaux-Arts. One is reminded of the ironic description that Hector Berlioz, a Prix de Rome winner himself in 1830, left behind:

> Every year, at the same day, the same hour, standing on the same steps of the same stairway of the Institut, the same academician utters the same phrase to the prizewinner who has just been crowned . . . : "Come now, young man, *macte animo* [have courage]; you are going on a beautiful voyage . . . the classic land of the Fine Arts . . . an inspirational sky. . . . You are on a beautiful path." For this glorious day the academicians put on their fine vestment embroidered with green; they shine forth, bedazzle. They are about to crown a painter, sculptor, architect, engraver, and musician all at once. Great is the joy at the gynaeceum of the muses.[9]

The prizewinners, most often between twenty and thirty years old, departed as a group at the beginning of December, arriving in Rome in early January. In his *Itinéraire d'un voyage de Paris à Rome, dédié aux pensionnaires de l'Académie de France à Rome* (1869), Charles Garnier recommends setting aside thirty days—even if twenty-seven might suffice—to visit the principal cities on the way to Rome. He estimates the cost of travel to be 700 francs "if one lived comfortably and if one did not haggle over prices too much; but in such a case, it would be quite possible for the young men to travel for 600 francs [the amount of the travel allowance allocated to the *pensionnaires*]. In spending 800 francs, one would travel like the English."[10] The voyage, by land or sea, was rather long and trying (notably in its sea crossings) and the arrival in Rome was at times disappointing. Dominique Papety wrote to his parents:

> At noon we caught our first glimpse of Saint Peter's dome. I prayed to God and the Virgin, as fervently as I could, asking them to grant me their protection during my stay in Rome. The weather was gray; it was raining; two hours later we entered into Rome proper. . . . Traversing the city, sadness came over me in seeing the city in such a sorry state. It was our misfortune that we passed through the worst neighborhoods; since it was Sunday, everything was closed. While traveling, always by coach, we saw the colonnade of Saint Peter's, which seemed to us excessively small. Finally we arrived at the Academy, our hearts beating fiercely. Mr. Ingres received us cordially, took us on a tour of the principal rooms of the villa, and then we dined. The *pensionnaires* received us with a great show of friendship. There was much to talk about, and everyone has something to say here and never tires of it. In the next few days I will begin my visits. I can assure you that, as of now, I desire nothing else in the world. A man could scarcely be more satisfied than I am right now. I will not stop repeating it: I find Rome the only habitable place on earth.[11]

Here is just one among many observations: orange trees laden with fruit in the dead of winter amazed these children of the North, *pensionnaires* and visiting artists alike. "Above all, the orange trees, majestic in their surroundings, laden with their nearly ripe fruits, delight me," raved Gustave Moreau.[12] Auguste Ottin offered a more materialistic point of view, judging that "the orange tree brings in as much as the apple tree. Thus you should think that the orange tree is a bit more beautiful than the apple tree."[13]

The place was always bewitching. As Michel-Martin Drolling wrote his father on June 11, 1811:

> The boarding school is [in] a wonderful palazzo, completely isolated and very well situated; it dominates the entire city since it is quite elevated, contributing to the fact that the air is very pure. I went straightaway to my room, which had been ready for several days since they were expecting us. My studio, big and quite beautiful, is right next to my room. I have a view of the gardens and the mansion, which is magnificent, as well as on the beautiful Roman countryside. It is the most marvelous sight that one can imagine . . . every day I have it before my eyes. My studio as well as my room face the setting sun every evening; I see the sun set behind the mountains and often there are spectacular effects. Ah, it is certainly the homeland of the arts. Every step that one takes, one is in a state of admiration, in an ecstasy that leaves you speechless.[14]

One's arrival, however, could be met with unexpected moments, marked by schoolboy pranks and jokes, especially at the end of the term. "We spent the entire evening and night in the midst of a throng of hearty fellows, happy to see new faces, and no less happy to renew old, established traditions.[15] They made us dine under atrocious conditions, on a table without a tablecloth, lit only by two measly smoky candles, all in order to give us a dreadful idea of the life that we were about to enjoy. That meager table's filth nevertheless interested me because I noticed a number of names—which had since become famous—carved with a knife into the wood."[16] The settling into one's room and studio, the introductions to the director and to the other *pensionnaires,* the discovery of the charms of the villa's gardens, the first letter sent to or received from one's loved ones back in France—all were very intense experiences for these young men who, more often than not, had left their native cities, or at least their native country, for the first time; by means of the quill or the paintbrush they sought to preserve the memory of these moments or to conjure up the emotions or feelings associated with them. [See, for example, the painting by Léon Cogniet, p. 19.]

REGULATIONS

The regulations, however, rapidly found their proper place once again, and in this splendid yet austere setting life went on just like in a boarding school—with one recurring problem: married students. In principle regulations forbade it, but as soon as the Academy opened in the Villa Medici, this problem, linked to that of age limits, presented itself: "When will the maximum allowable age at the school be set? What end does it serve to send men here who are approaching fifty years of age or who, at the very least, are older than forty, who leave behind in Paris [because the trip would have been too expensive] their wives and children in frightful misery?"[17] The problem resurfaced under the directorships of Horace Vernet and Jean Auguste Dominique Ingres with respect to Frédéric Schopin, Eugène Prévost, Victor Baltard, and Auguste Ottin, who were already married before having won the Grand Prix, while Jean-Arnaud Léveil and Pierre-Joseph Garrez married in Rome. As Vernet remarked, one had to decide if the Academy was "a school for young men called forth to develop their skills through participation in competitions, or a means for men with proven talents to perfect them. In the first case, the rules are insufficient, and in the second, they are not applicable to thirty-five-year-old artists who have already enjoyed their freedom and who often have familial responsibilities to fulfill."[18] But the Académie des Beaux-Arts, in the person of its permanent secretary Antoine Quatremère de Quincy, did not agree with the director and reminded the *pensionnaires,* in no uncertain terms, to better appreciate their situation. "What does obtaining the Grand Prix, by the approbation of the Academy, bestow [upon the artist]? The right to continue their studies in Rome in a more rarefied sphere. What are the compulsory exercises imposed on the students and what are they called? These exercises are called *études* and are indeed "studies." But to undertake studies required by the regulations and submitted to the criticisms of the Academy according to these same regulations, doesn't that—vis-à-vis the Academy in a state . . . that, in all the superior stages of

all the great institutions of higher learning—constitute the status of the student and justify it in every sense of the word?"[19] "You have an uncommon opinion of the *pensionnaires,*" complained Léon Vaudoyer to his father during this same period. "You think that it is just as it was in your day, that they are held in great esteem, that one attaches great importance to their talents, that one would be inclined to let them create something. Not at all. It's nothing like that. They are still considered pupils who are studying and who are not yet able to practice their art."[20]

During the five years that they spent in Rome, the *pensionnaires* had to submit an *envoi* every year to Paris. The nature of these compulsory exercises, whose progress was supposed to reflect that of their studies, remained unchanged during their entire stay. The studious *pensionnaire* "always had to bear in mind the required task of demonstrating in each of his works progress in drawing, mastery of the nude, the correction of forms, and [a belief] in that truth of imitative perfection which expression reveals and which the artist increasingly strives to perfect throughout his career, without regard to limitations."[21] Painters thus had to submit the following: for the first three years a life-size nude figure painted from a live model (the requirement of four nude figures—two drawn from nature and the other two drawn from the antique—as well as a sketch of a painted or drawn composition being neither respected nor required); for the fourth year a copy of an old master painting of the *pensionnaire*'s choice; and for the fifth year a history painting of his choice, measuring 325 centimeters [128 inches] in height (in his fourth year the *pensionnaire* often sent a sketch of his composition to elicit the advice of the Institut). For their part, during their stay in Rome sculptors had to execute—in a sequence that changed—a marble copy of an antique statue of their choice; plaster models of a sculpture in the round at least half life-size; a life-size bas-relief figure sculpted from life; at least one head in the round, one study in the round whose size had to be at least 33–38 centimeters [13–15 inches]; and, finally, a study of a nude life-size figure of their choice and its translation into marble. As was the case under the ancien régime, the copies were the property of the government, along with the fifth-year *envois,* "destined to give credit to the French School and to be placed in the special museum for this school at Versailles if they are judged worthy." In 1821, however, it was decided that these works would remain the property of the artists: exhibited at the Salon in Paris, often purchased by the state, many of these works marked the beginning of their author's career. Copies after the antique (the basis of studies according to the decree of 1799),[22] the extolling of the study from nature: the *École de Rome* was very much a continuation of the École des Beaux-Arts and remained faithful to the aesthetic precepts already in place.

The *envois* were a subject of concern for the director as well as for the *pensionnaires*. The early directors—through the directorship of Pierre-Narcisse Guérin (1823–28)—had great difficulty in ascertaining that the works were done in the time allotted. Nevertheless, they had at their disposal a method of coercion, namely, the *retenue* [withholding]: 25 francs were withheld each month from the stipend of 200 francs that each *pensionnaire* received (this was increased to 230 francs during the second term of Jean-Victor Schnetz's directorship [1853–65]), to be returned at the time of the student's departure only if he had satisfied his obligations. Even if a greater sense of conformity in the works had crept in over time, there were always delinquent *pensionnaires*, who submitted their projects late or whose subject matter did not fulfill the requirements. For example, instead of the proscribed figure, Jean-Baptiste Carpeaux proposed for his last year (1859) a group entitled *Ugolino*, which necessitated that he stay in Rome one more year than anticipated.

As soon as he had settled in, the young painter or sculptor busied himself with his first *envoi*. "I think that I will not delay in getting to work," Drolling wrote to his father in a letter dated May 3, 1811, where he recounts his arrival, "because I have to do a figure by the end of August." Baudry, having arrived in Rome on January 28, sent a missive to his parents, dated March 9, 1851, in which he wrote: "I still don't have a studio. I won't have one until the end of April, at which time I will begin the painting that will be exhibited in Paris in 1852."[23] Indeed, the works were presented in Rome in the fall for the first exhibition (1805), then again in April,[24] before being sent to Paris, with paintings and architectural projects shipped by land and sculpture by sea. In the fall they were exhibited at the École des Beaux-Arts and submitted to the scrutiny of the public (the press reviewed them as well),[25] and above all to that of the Académie des Beaux-Arts, meaning the masters of the *pensionnaires*, since everyone knew that in order to win the Prix de Rome it was better to have learned sound principles from a member of the Institut. (Carpeaux had not hesitated to transfer from François Rude's studio to that of Francisque Duret, which enabled him to win the Grand Prix de Rome in 1854.) The permanent secretary (Joachim Le Breton, then Antoine Quatremère de Quincy, Désiré Raoul-Rochette, and Louis Halévy) summarized the observations of the different sections in a "report" in which the works were analyzed in detail in terms of both their form and execution as well as their expression of ideas and feelings, and were criticized—at times severely—especially if the Institut suspected a desire to "produce" flashy effects. This report was read in October during the annual public session of the Academy, and was then sent to the director of the *École de Rome*. The *pensionnaires* anxiously awaited the report, its reading by the director constituting one of the highlights of the year. "At last my *Philoctetes* will be on its way to Paris in two days at the latest," wrote Drolling to his father on September 7, 1814. "I cannot wait to receive your advice; write as soon as you have seen it. I also beg you to go to Mr. David to find out what he thinks. I am showing my painting to Mr. Lethière [then director of the Academy]; he seemed fairly pleased by its composition and by what has already been done." "Have you written to your brother?" asked a worried Ingres of Auguste Flandrin concerning his brother Hippolyte's *envoi* [*Polites*; see p. 27] about which he initially had had a negative impression. "Don't do it; my decision was unjust. It's better, much better. These gentlemen [of the Institut] saw it and the report will be favorable. Don't say anything to this poor boy; it would make him sick. I shall soon speak to him."[26] Everyone, however, did not take things to heart. "Mr. Duret will not upset me," declared Henri Chapu coolly,[27] who had decided, like so many others, to follow his instinct for *Christ and the Angels* (1857, bas-relief, Musée Chapu, Le Mée). However, a letter written on October 10, 1857, while the *pensionnaires* were awaiting the report on the *envois*, suggests that he did indeed suspect that the report would not be too favorable and that he worried about it, even though he later claimed "not having any regrets about anything." Baudry confided the same thing to Marquerie: "It seems that my *Theseus* [first-year *envoi*] was judged severely, this despite your friendly words of encouragement. I received the written report and manuscript from the Institut, the latter being more detailed,[28] and I saw that my *Theseus* did not appear to be attractive enough to its members. Nevertheless, I frankly don't have too many complaints about this judgment: it contains some real truths, as Mr. [Adolphe] Thiers suggested, from which I will profit."[29] In a subsequent letter to his parents he wrote: "We have received news from the Institut concerning our works and here is what we know: M. Horace Vernet was asked to write the report on the paintings. This report was deemed so violent and unjust that the Institut decided that it should be modified and toned down. I think that all the newspapers that despise the Institut, the Academy, and all the rest are ready to pounce on us. It will be very amusing!"[30] The *envois* helped to create a sense of community among the *pensionnaires*, who passed judgment on each other, provided information to those who were absent, and collectively awaited the reaction from Paris. Thus, in a letter to Hippolyte Flandrin dated April 29, 1829, Dominique Papety provides details on the *envois* by the *pensionnaires*, ranging from painters to architects: "I'm going to try to tell you about everything that goes on here. First, our exhibition, which closes today, has attracted huge crowds, the nice weather having certainly contributed. I tell you that Roger's painting is much better than anything he has done up to now, and this has really made me happy. . . . Then come the architects, who, with the exception of [Auguste] Famin, have all done remarkable things. . . . Here it is, the austere *envoi*."[31]

The reception of the *envois* was all the more important for the *pensionnaires* because they incurred costs and did not necessarily have access to financial resources. "At the Villa Medici," writes Jean-Marie-Bienaimé Bonnassieux, "we have everything we need, everything that is necessary to satisfy our obligations, but one who does not have personal resources can do nothing beyond that. The hundred plus francs we receive per month are greatly reduced after we've paid our models (who are just as expensive as in Paris), our domestic servant, the Italian teacher, and provided for our upkeep. I'm speaking about the new *pensionnaires*. Later on one can do some work or sell some *envois*."[32] A bit later the same Bonnassieux was trying to make his bas-relief "appealing according to the fashions of the times" in order to sell it, which would allow him to "manage [his] studies more briskly."[33] Baudry, in turn, writes: "I truly have need of money if I am to make my stay in Italy profitable; with the 75 francs I receive each month from the state[34] it's impossible for me to make ends meet."[35] Thus, the *pensionnaires* tried to reconcile the requirements set forth in the regulations with the necessities of life, while at the same time attempting to create works—painted or sculpted—that might appeal to a clientele of art lovers. As Baudry wrote to Gustave Guitton: "My painting for this year [*The Fortune*] would, I believe, sell much more easily [than *Jacob Wrestling the Angel* (1852, Musée Municipal, La Roche-sur-Yon)]; but you won't be able to have it until October. For that one my hopes are much more ambitious: I want four to five thousand francs for it, but it's a golden dream."[36] As for sculptors, they were tempted to sculpt in marble and to sell the figures on the spot even if the regulations only asked for plaster models.

STUDIES

For the private room, as for the studio, the Academy provided the basics, the barest essentials. For example, if one examines the financial accounts of 1827,[37] one notices that the expenditures, excluding stipends, connected to the *pensionnaires* were allocated between "common expenses" and "expenses specific to studies." The former comprised "the school of the live model," the packing and shipment of works by the *pensionnaires*, and casts and purchases for the library; the latter expenditures corresponded to reimbursements of the costs of copies by Jean-Louis Desprez and Jean Debay, and of the restoration of the *Portico of Octavian* by Félix Duban. The following year the specific expenses were more substantial because of the acquisition of marble for copies by Jean-Louis Jaley and François Lanno, as well as for the fifth-year figure by Augustin Dumont, and to reimburse the first two for what the stone carver had cost them. The Academy was responsible for expenses incurred with respect to works that belonged to the state, copies by painters and sculptors, restoration drawings by architects, as well as the purchase of marble for statues executed during the sculptors' final year. In general, painters did not cost too much money. Architects sometimes asked for measured drawings that might necessitate the erection of scaffolding. But "it was the sculptors who were the most expensive," noted Pierre-Narcisse Guérin:[38] for the copy one had to make a cast of the original and then buy marble and pay for the *ébauche* [rudimentary stage of an artwork before completion], which was also the case for the figure for the final year. To take several examples, Court received 32.92 piastres for the painted copy he made after Valentin de Boulogne (June 17, 1823), while the figure sculpted by Georges Jacquot came to 233.83 piastres (for purchase, transport, and "placement" of the marble; October 12, 1825); that by Philippe Lemaire was 130 piastres for the purchase of the marble from the sculptor Kessels (August 10, 1825), to which were added 46.66 piastres for the transport, placement, and sawing of this marble (October 1, 1826); and the copy by Jean-Louis Desprez, not counting the purchase of the marble, came to 132.10 piastres. During the same period, François Villain received 32.10 piastres for his restoration drawings of the *Temple of Marcus Aurelius* (July 14, 1825), and Abel Blouet was paid 107.06 piastres for that of the *Baths of Caracalla* (October 10, 1825).[39]

Similar to the École des Beaux-Arts, the two types of drawing—after antique statuary and after the live model— held an important position. In 1826 Guérin could complain all he wanted that "the school of modeling and the antique gallery remained deserted."[40] He no sooner reprimanded his *pensionnaires* than the financial accounts clearly showed the importance attached to them. The Academy thus placed one model (who changed every month) at the disposal of the young artists. "The live and nude model will be placed in one of the rooms of the palazzo, specially designated for such a study, every day for two hours, with the exception of the days of rest as prescribed by law. This study will take place between six and eight in the morning during the six summer months and from six in the evening until eight during the six winter months, " as provided for in the ruling of the Year VII (1799).[41] The room located immediately to the left of the vestibule on the street level was dedicated to sittings: we know from financial accounts that it had to be heated until June, that lighting had to be provided (oil lamps and "a little candle with which to light them") from November to May, and that in September and October the sessions ended. This "School of the Nude" or "Evening Academy," as it is often called—as early as the 1830s and perhaps even earlier, these sessions were held only in the evening—were open to outside artists, as was the case in the Palazzo Mancini in the 18th century; Gustave Moreau and Edgar Degas profited greatly from them. The *pensionnaires* themselves also went to draw at the Academy of Saint Luke [the Italian art academy in Rome], where public modeling sessions had been held since 1754[42] and where models were listed elsewhere on the list of "tips" for the same amount (100 francs) as the "house model." For their *envois* they nevertheless had to resort to personal models, which they hired on the Piazza d'Espagna, where professional models gathered,[43] or by chance while walking around—unless, that is, they had them brought down from Paris, as Henri Regnault did [for his *Judith and Holophernes* (1869), Musée des Beaux-Arts, Marseille].

The drawing from the live nude model was matched by the drawing after antique statuary and Old Masters. It was possible to practice very well on location since the Academy owned an important collection of casts, with the sculptures being presented in the gallery on the main floor of the *pensionnaires'* wing and the architectural casts and fragments in a contiguous gallery under the footbridge that Ingres had ordered built in 1838. Suvée had poured all of his energy into reconstituting this collection, which was also accessible to outside artists. Some of the works had come from the Palazzo Mancini, and the collection was enriched as the century progressed. Unfortunately, it suffered considerably as a result of the 20th century's contempt for casts, and today only a small portion of it

survives, in mediocre condition, and regrettably is seldom on display. The list of tips reveals that the *pensionnaires* also frequented other places, underscoring the esteem in which these places were held (or, perhaps, the difficulty that one found in working there?). The Vatican was first in line: the "caretaker of the paintings of Raphael" actually received 600 francs and that of the Museo Clementino 400, while those of the Capitol, of the Albani museum, and of the Farnesina only made 200, and the commissioner of the Villa Borghese and the beadle of the Academy of Saint Luke 50. Gustave Moreau, who had come to Rome at his own expense, provides a very instructive basis of comparison. He draws up an account of the "good hands that monthly had to give to these fierce doorkeepers of galleries."[44] Long after his return to Paris, Henri Chapu also recalled with nostalgia "that wonderful time when we went to measure and study the antique works of the Gallery at the Academy in Rome, the museums, galleries, studies, and sketches that we amassed, and that I don't even have the time to see again."[45] Indeed, he [Moreau] spent part of his Sunday mornings "measuring the proportions of the beautiful antique statues."[46] The *pensionnaires* completed the working sessions in situ by taking tracings, especially from the collection of vases to which they had access in the library of the Villa, and, later, through photographs. Thus, the *pensionnaires* assembled an invaluable repertory of forms and ideas, as exemplified in the Henri Chapu collection at Melun, the two albums of sculptor Jean-Joseph Perraud in the Museum of Lons-le-Saunier,[47] or the collection of photographs after Raphael gathered by Jean-Baptiste Deschamps (Musée Greuze, Tournus), all of which constitute very typical examples.

TRIPS

Trips permitted the *pensionnaires* to add another dimension to their studies. From early on, following the example of Pierre-Henri de Valenciennes and with the encouragement of Nicolas-Didier Boguet or François-Marius Granet, the painters looked for the "background of paintings" in the vicinity of Rome. On September 22, 1813, Drolling wrote to his father: "I will tell you that the landscape of my *Death of Abel* is tormenting me very much. These next few days I am going to explore the environs of Rome to try to discover something that suits me." Director Guérin recognized that one of the most useful contributions of the Roman sojourn was for artists to assemble a collection of studies after nature and character types, as well as picturesque motifs or landscapes. Augustin Dumont, who had listened attentively, in turn recommended to Bonnassieux that he collect these "very useful materials" since he would-n't find their equal in Paris. Bonnassieux heeded him, as his letters to Dumont attest,[48] for he crisscrossed the Latium [the region around Rome] before venturing to the north, toward Florence, and to the south, toward Naples and Sicily.

During the first two years the regulations forbade the *pensionnaires* to wander more than forty miles outside of Rome. During this period and even afterward—especially during the summer months in order to escape the yellow fever prevalent in Rome's humid climate—they made excursions in the Latium lasting several days. They left in small groups, with portfolios under their arms, a painter or a sculptor accompanying an architect intending to execute a measured drawing or a composer seeking inspiration. A few months after his arrival, Francisque Duret allowed himself to be guided by Dumont, Paul Dubois, and Édouard Boilly to Subiaco, Palestrina, and Albano; but no sooner had they passed Tivoli than Duret—sick and tired of the tedious trip, walking under a hot sun, and in a bad mood following a quarrel with his friends—decided to enter a coach and return to Rome. Despite [sculptor] Denis Foyatier's assurances to the contrary, he obviously did not have "the art of travel under his belt."[49] On the other hand, several years later Dominique Papety provided an idyllic description of the same:

> wonderful Roman countryside that no one will ever be able to describe and that one must absolutely see before dying. . . . It is here that one finds herds of white cows and their herdsmen hidden under a hut for protection against the sun; it's here that he sleeps, it's here that he spends his life contemplating the sky, slowly repeating the song of the Madonna, which does one's soul so much good. All these pastures and beautiful Sabine hills transport you to biblical times; one can almost see the beautiful Ruth lying at the feet of Boaz or the young Joseph looking for his brothers. At times these hills become wilder, and one can almost see Cain fleeing in the distance without being able to escape the anger of a vengeful god.[50]

The same excursion is described by Hippolyte Flan-drin in his diary in a more succinct manner but with the same enthusiasm, as well as in his sketches: "April 19. Actors: Boulanger, Farochon, Papety, Paul and myself. Departure at 7 in the morning. The weather is horrible. . . . We climb to Tivoli on foot under a prickly sun, precursor to rain. Arriving at the Sibyl, we are enchanted by every-thing that we see: everything appears to me to be more beautiful than in reality."[51] Thanks to more flexible regula-tions, the scope of these trips widened as the century pro-gressed; the *pensionnaires* were given the chance to visit Venice or Sicily, then Greece, and to copy Trecento or Quattrocento masters in Pisa or Florence.

## THE SCHOOL AND THE VILLA

Although no *pensionnaire* questioned the usefulness of the Italian sojourn, the school's regulations were difficult to accept by artists who had already frequently exhibited their works at the Salon and who had garnered favorable press reviews. With art increasingly falling under the purview of the public sphere and not of the Academy, and with careers developing with critics in mind rather than in the studio, the *pensionnaires* remained reticent and skepti-cal when confronted with the necessity of continuing their studies in Rome after having been awarded prizes at com-petitions. Thus, in 1826 Guérin complained of their casual attitude toward regulations: "The word study seems to wound their self-esteem, and such is the current trend that, above all else, one must produce dazzling effects. It is the only goal, and the conscientious execution of required fig-ures is thus seen as a waste of time and sacrificed to the desire to churn out compositions."[52]

Without invoking the problems of academic norms or the ideology of the avant-garde, it is evident that the artis-tic foundation of the *École* is the continuation of a tradi-tion, of the preeminence of a certain type of history painting or classical sculpture, of models from the past, or of the examples of the great masters. In this sense, the *École* was certainly a success: it not only facilitated the explosion of talent in artists like Hippolyte Flandrin, Pierre-Charles Simart, Jean-Joseph Perraud, Adolphe-William Bouguereau, and Louis Barrias; it also made possible the formation of a school, of a relatively homogeneous artistic language whose conventions evolved as the century pro-gressed. One should also stress the fact that thanks to the ability of its directors and to its geographic distance, the institution was flexible enough to welcome and support mavericks such as Ingres, Court, Carpeaux, and Regnault. We conclude with a reflection of former *pensionnaires* and eyewitnesses to history: the Villa is a powerful place and the possibilities of contact and of greater independence that it offers certainly influence the mind—even more so, undoubtedly, those of 19th-century provincials who were perhaps less up to date and knowledgeable prior to their Roman emancipation of the larger trends and of the appeal of the artistic life. For the Marseillais Dominique Papety, who at the beginning of his stay wanted to strictly abide by the regulations, the villa was a place marked by open-mindedness and rupture: in his correspondence friends end up almost totally replacing parents, and his last letters show his emancipation from the authorities: "My social desires have changed; art is no longer my only idol; another has come to rest on the scale—that of Fortune. . . . I hold art in high esteem and still love it very much; notwithstanding what I am about to tell you, it is still my favorite pastime, but I love the life of ease. I would love to fulfill all my desires of luxury and love."[54] To Ottin, Papety confessed: "As for me, I have divorced myself from the Academy. I live below [in the city], eat at Lepre, and sleep at 14, Via Pinciana."[55]

## NOTES

1. Baudelaire, 1859, quoted in Philippe Grunchec, *Les concours des prix de Rome, 1797–1863*, 2 vols., 2nd ed., with a preface by Jacques Thuillier (Paris, 1989), vol. 1, p. 19.

2. Report by Guinguené to the Comité d'Instruction publique, October 18, 1795, quoted in *Correspondance des directeurs de l'Académie de France à Rome. Nouvelle série. Directorat de Jean-Benoît Suvée, 1795–1807*, 2 vols., ed. George Brunel and Isabelle Julia (Rome, 1984), vol. 1, p. 55.

3. On November 20, 1792, Suvée had already been named director of a French Academy in Rome that was suppressed five days later.

4. *Correspondance des directeurs . . . Suvée*, vol. 1, p. 61.

5. *Correspondance des directeurs de l'Académie de France à Rome avec les surintendants des Bâtiments*, 18 vols., ed. Anatole de Montaiglon and Jules Guiffrey (Paris, 1857–1908), vol. 17, pp. 190–97.

6. On the creation in 1803 of the prizes for musical composition, medal engraving, and line engraving, see Cécile Reynaud, "La création du grand prix de Rome de composition musicale: l'Institut, l'Académie de France à Rome et les premiers pensionnaires compositeurs" (pp. 3–14), and Jean Guillemin, "La section de gravure en médailles à la Villa Médicis (1805–1970)" (pp. 15–46), in *L'Académie de France à Rome aux XIXe et XXe siècles: Entre tradition, modernité et création*, Collection d'histoire de l'art de l'Académie de France à Rome, 2 (Paris and Rome, 2002).

7. Article 2, title 3, of the regulation of April 4, 1799, in *Correspondance des directeurs . . . Suvée*, vol. 1, p. 164.

8. See Henri Lapauze, *Histoire de l'Académie de France à Rome*, 2 vols. (Paris, 1924), vol. 2, p. 9.

9. Hector Berlioz, *Mémoires, comprenant ses voyages en Italie, en Allemagne, en Russie et en Angleterre, 1803–1865* (Paris, 1881), vol. 1, pp. 161–62.

10. Manuscript in the library of the Paris Opéra, Garnier holdings.

11. Letter dated January 30, 1837, quoted in François-Xavier Amprimoz, "Lettres de Dominique Papety à ses parents et ses amis, Rome, 1837–1842," *Archives de l'Art français* 28 (1986): 205.

12. Letter to his parents dated November 20, 1857, quoted in Luisa Capodieci, *Gustave Moreau: Correspondance d'Italie* (Paris, 2002), p. 87.

13. Letter dated March 1, 1837, quoted in Antoinette Le Normand, *La tradition classique et l'esprit romantique: Les sculpteurs de l'Académie de France à Rome de 1824 à 1840* (Rome, 1981), p. 101.

14. The correspondence between the history painter and Prix de Rome laureate Michel-Martin Drolling and his father, Michel Drolling, who specialized in interiors, is located in the Département des arts graphiques at the Musée du Louvre (L1 to L168), to which all subsequent references refer. This correspondence is most interesting, for it contains not only the letters sent by the *pensionnaire* but also those from his father, which he received from Paris.

15. The walls of the dining room of the *pensionnaires* were, in fact, covered with caricatures of the *pensionnaires* and their portraits, generally painted by the painter following his promotion at the end of his fifth year of residence in Rome.

16. Letter by Paul Baudry to Gustave Guitton, quoted in Charles Ephrussi, *Paul Baudry, sa vie et son oeuvre* (Paris, 1887), p. 73. Here is a similar account by Jules Massenet regarding his first dinner at the villa: "The old ones all had a roguish physique, which did not prevent them, at a given moment, from telling us that even though the food was simple, one lived here in the greatest fraternal harmony. Suddenly, following a lively artistic discussion, discord set in and one saw all the plates and bottles fly through the air amid loud cries. . . . Even though we knew we were being teased, I was slightly taken aback. Not daring to move, I lowered my head and read the name of Hérold, which the author of *Le pré aux clercs* had engraved there with his knife when he was a *pensionnaire* at this same Villa Medici." Quoted in *Jules Massenet: Mes souvenirs, 1848–1912* (Paris, 1912), pp. 42–43.

17. Suvée to Le Breton, August 28, 1805, in *Correspondance des directeurs . . . Suvée*, vol. 2, no. 588, p. 687.

18. Vernet to the Minister, May 22, 1832, quoted in Lapauze, *Histoire de l'Académie de France à Rome*, vol. 2, p. 212.

19. Quatremère de Quincy's remarks dated June 30, 1830, quoted in Lapauze, *Histoire de l'Académie de France à Rome*, vol. 2, p. 194.

20. Vaudoyer's remarks dated April 28, 1830. Paris, Private Collection.

21. Report on the works of 1826, Archives de l'Académie de France à Rome, Villa Medici, carton 30.

22. *Correspondance des directeurs . . . Suvée*, vol. 1, no. 67, pp. 158–69.

23. Quoted in Ephrussi, *Paul Baudry*, p. 74.

24. Distinguished visitors often came to see the works of the *pensionnaires* in their studios, before the opening of the exhibition, with or without the director. See, for example, the letter by Papety to his parents dated April 28, 1838, quoted in Amprimoz, "Lettres de Dominique Papety," pp. 230–31.

25. See Neil McWilliam, "Exercises de style: La critique d'art devant les envois de Rome," in *Maestà di Roma. D'Ingres à Degas: Les artistes français à Rome*, exh. cat., Rome, Villa Médicis (Milan, 2003), pp. 139–49.

26. Letter from Auguste to Hippolyte Flandrin, August 15, 1834, quoted in Louis Flandrin, *Hippolyte Flandrin, sa vie et son oeuvre* (Paris, 1902), pp. 50–51.

27. Letter to his parents dated May 24, 1856, in the Musée Municipal, Melun.

28. The written report either corresponds to the printed report or to the copy of the minutes, which is often softened in comparison to the nonofficial written version transmitted to the director of the École des Beaux-Arts in Paris. The series of minutes, together with the official reports, are in the archives of the Institut (Archives de l'Académie des Beaux-Arts, Institut de France, Paris, series 2E).

29. Letter dated December 29, 1852, quoted in Ephrussi, *Paul Baudry*, p. 103.

30. Letter dated September 31, 1853, quoted in Ephrussi, *Paul Baudry*, p. 126.

31. Quoted in Amprimoz, "Lettres de Dominique Papety," p. 248.

32. Letter to his parents dated June 3, 1837, quoted in Léo Armagnac, *Bonnassieux, sa vie et son oeuvre* (Paris, 1897), p. 36.

33. Bonnassieux to Dumont, September 5, 1838, quoted in Gaston Brière, "Notes et documents: Relevé des autographes intéressant l'histoire des arts en France passes en vente. II: 1921–1922," *Bulletin de la Société de l'Histoire de l'Art français* (1923): 339.

34. Of the 200 francs comprising the monthly allowance, 100 were withheld for food and 25 for lodging: leaving only 75 to the pensionnaire for daily expenses, which, according to Bizet, was further subdivided as follows: laundry, 5 francs; wood, candle, and stamp, 10 francs; gloves and servants, 5 francs; communal fund, 15 francs; lastly 15 francs for the piano or 1.5 francs per hour for the models, not counting the paper, pencils, etcetera. Cited in Lapauze, *Histoire de l'Académie de France à Rome*, vol. 2, p. 348. Note that while reconciling his accounts six months after his arrival in Rome, a trip undertaken at his own expense, Gustave Moreau figured that he had spent 1,100 francs: "In six months that's a little less than 200 francs per month" Letter dated April

28, 1858, quoted in Capodieci, *Gustave Moreau*, p. 331. A bit later he specified that his lodging in Rome cost 80 francs per month, which almost equaled a trip by carriage from Rome to Florence (72 francs, plus 15 francs for visas).

35. Letter to his parents dated March 9, 1852, quoted in Ephrussi, *Paul Baudry,* p. 90.
36. Letter dated July 2, 1854, quoted in Ephrussi, *Paul Baudry,* p. 132. The "most he could hope" for *Jacob Wrestling the Angel* was two thousand francs. But Baudry disapproved of exhibiting his *envoi* at a dealer's (p. 134).
37. Archives de l'Académie de France à Rome, Villa Medici, box 33.
38. Guérin to the Minister of the Interior, March 18, 1829, Archives nationales de France, Paris, F21 589.
39. These receipts are located in the Archives de l'Académie de France à Rome, Villa Medici, box 32, labeled "*comptes.*"
40. *Tableau des envois de 1826;* the original, in Paris, is housed in the Archives de l'Académie des Beaux-Arts, 5E17.
41. *Correspondance des directeurs . . . Suvée,* vol 1, no. 67, p. 160.
42. See the symposium paper by Olivier Michel entitled "La formation des artistes étrangers à Rome: Leur présence à l'"Accademia del nudo' de 1754 à 1800" ["L'Educazione dell'uomo e della donna nella cultura illuministica / L'Éducation de l'homme et da la femme au XVIIIe siècle," symposium held at the Accademia delle Scienze, Turin, October 16–18, 1997], *Memorie dell'Accademia delle Scienze di Torino, Classe di Scienze morali, storiche e filologiche,* 5, vol. 24, no. 3 (2000): 279–85.
43. That is where Regnault found a model for his *Salomé;* see André Beaunier, *Les souvenirs d'un peintre* [Georges Clairin] (Paris, 1906), p. 101.
44. Letter to his parents dated April 28, 1858, quoted in Capodieci, *Gustave Moreau,* p. 331.
45. Chapu to Gustave Moreau, January 15, 1880, in Musée Gustave Moreau, Paris.
46. Letter to his parents dated January 20, 1858, quoted in Capodieci, *Gustave Moreau,* p. 205.
47. For an account of the excellent work performed by Christiane Dotal with respect to the loan registers of the library of the Villa Medici, see her "Jean-Joseph Perraud (1819–1876) et la sculpture néo-classique sous le second Empire," (Ph.D. diss., University of Bourgogne, Dijon, 2002), pp. 43–49.
48. Bonnassieux to Dumont, July 8, 1837, and December 3, 1841, quoted in Le Normand, *La tradition classique et l'esprit romantique,* pp. 146 and 181, resp.
49. Letter from Duret to his motherdated September 1824, quoted in Le Normand, *La tradition classique et l'esprit romantique,* pp. 72–73.
50. Letter from Papety to his parents dated June 1837, quoted in Amprimoz, "Lettres de Dominique Papety," p. 211.
51. Marthe Flandrin et Madeleine Froidevaux-Flandrin, *Les frères Flandrin. Trois jeunes peintres au XIXe siècle. Leur correspondance. Le Journal inédit d'Hippolyte en Italie* (Paris, 1984), p. 102.
52. Guérin to Quatremère de Quincy, July 1, 1826, in the Archives de l'Académie de France à Rome, Villa Medici, box 30.
53. The expression and the concept "maverick" is borrowed from Howard S. Becker, *Art Worlds* (Berkeley, Calif., 1982), pp. 226–71.
54. Letter to Hippolyte Flandrin dated August 28, 1840, quoted in Amprimoz, "Lettres de Dominique Papety," p. 260.
55. Letter dated March 8, 1842, quoted in Amprimoz, "Lettres de Dominique Papety," p. 267.

# I.   THE VILLA MEDICI: A WORLD APART

The success of the French Academy in Rome during the 19th century depended not only upon the support of political leaders and intellectuals, such as the French ambassador in Rome François-René de Chateaubriand (1768–1848), but also on its extraordinary site. The Villa Medici, a marvelous Renaissance palazzo near the Spanish Steps that overlooks the entire city, dominated the cultural landscape both literally and figuratively. In addition to the many painters, sculptors, engravers, musicians and architects who lived and studied there, the Academy was frequented by such diverse visitors as the composer Franz Liszt (1811–1886) and the liberal Dominican priest Jean-Baptiste Lacordaire (1802–1861). The festivities organized at the Villa became legendary. This animated artistic and intellectual center introduced wide-ranging modern currents of thought to the Pontifical capital. Yet, perched atop a hill, the Villa was also a somewhat isolated universe, enjoying its own rhythm of life.

*Portraits*

It was a tradition for the *pensionnaires* (resident artists at the Villa Medici) to make portraits of themselves or their fellow students (below and p. 22), and every departing director was immortalized through a bust (p. 21). Most students also wished to keep a souvenir of their passage through this artistic paradise by representing themselves in their studio with a background view of modern Rome (p. 19). The enchanting site of the Villa Medici itself, its gardens and nearby monuments were frequent sources of inspiration for these painters.

SALOMON CORRODI
Fehraltonf (Switzerland) 1810–Como 1892
*View of the Villa Medici and Gardens,*
1844
Black ink and watercolor on paper,
30 x 45 cm [11¾ x 17¾ in.]
New York, Didier Aaron, Inc.

Built around 1540 by Annibale Lippi for Cardinal Ricci da Montepulciano, this palace was bought in 1576 by Ferdinando dei Medici, who later became the Grand Duke of Tuscany. The architect Ammannati modified the building for the Medici, who housed there their famous collection of ancient Roman sculptures (now in the Uffizi Gallery in Florence). In 1801, Napoleon acquired this so-called Villa Medici and the French Academy in Rome opened there in 1803.

The Villa Medici is famous for its inner façade onto the garden, decorated with numerous ancient Roman statues, medallions, columns and bas-reliefs. From the formal garden, the dome of St Peter's basilica dominates the view over Rome. The protruding wing on the left from the main building contained many of the artists' studios, such as the one occupied by Léon Cogniet (p. 19). Other artists' studios were in the towers of the main building, as well as in various buildings in the garden.

ADOLPHE-WILLIAM
BOUGUEREAU
La Rochelle 1825–La Rochelle 1905
*Pensionnaire*, 1830–1834
*Self-portrait*, 1854
Oil on canvas, 47 x 36 cm [18½ x 14³⁄₁₆ in.]
Rome, Académie de France

**ACHILLE-ETNA MICHALLON**
Paris 1796–Paris 1822
  *Pensionnaire*, 1818–1821
*View of the Villa Medici through an Arch*,
ca. 1818
Oil on paper, adhered to canvas,
22 x 29.5 cm [8⅝ x 11⅜ in.]
Orléans, Musée des Beaux-Arts

In 1817, Michallon was the first winner of
the *prix de Rome* for Historical Landscape, a category conceived the previous

year. In this charming and informal picture, Michallon framed his view of the
northern façade of the Villa Medici, as
seen from the Borghese gardens, using the
common pictorial device of looking
through an archway in the foreground.

**LÉON COGNIET**
Paris 1794–Paris 1880
  *Pensionnaire*, 1818–1822
*The Fountain Basin of the Villa Medici in
Rome, at Night*, not dated

Oil on paper, adhered to canvas,
20 x 23 cm [7⅞ x 9 in.]
Orléans, Musée des Beaux-Arts

The famous fountain basin in front of the
Villa Medici was a favorite subject for
many *pensionnaires*. Everyone exiting
through the villa's front door is greeted by
this large stone dish, called a *vasque*,
marking the spectacular view of Rome
behind it.

## JEAN AUGUSTE DOMINIQUE INGRES
Montauban 1780–Paris 1867
 *Pensionnaire*, 1805–1810
 Director of the Villa Medici, 1835–1840
*François-Marius Granet*, 1807–1809
Oil on canvas, 74.5 x 63.2 cm
[29⅜ x 24⅞ in.]
Aix-en-Provence, Musée Granet

Although not a *prix de Rome* winner, Granet lived primarily in Rome from 1802 to 1824. He became close friends with Ingres when the latter was a *pensionnaire* at the Villa Medici. Dressed in a painter's cape with a sketchbook in hand, Granet is depicted against the dramatic backdrop of the Quirinal Palace before an approaching storm.

In 1835, years after this portrait was painted, Granet wrote to Ingres, who had just become Director of the Villa Medici: "Promise me to sometimes think of your old friend in this beautiful classical land, where I have spent the sweetest moments of my life. When you are with our [painter Nicolas-Didier] Boguet, exclaim together: if only Granet were here!"

## LÉON COGNIET
Paris 1794–Paris 1880
*Pensionnaire*, 1818–1822
*The Artist in his Room at the Villa Medici,*
1818
Oil on canvas, 44.5 x 37 cm [17½ x 14⅝ in.]
Cleveland Museum of Art

As noted in an inscription on the reverse
of this canvas, Cogniet painted this self-
portrait to commemorate the first letter he
received from his family. That he chose to
depict this touching moment is not sur-
prising. His trip from France to Rome
probably took him approximately two
months and upon departure he knew he
would not see his relatives for the next
five years. As is known from his letters,
the landscape seen through the open window attests to the artist's preference for
painting outdoors.

Although Cogniet was expected to study
history painting during his Roman sojourn,
his true passion lay in discovering his
exotic new environment. In 1818, the
artist wrote to his teacher Pierre-Narcisse
Guérin: "You ask me, what strikes me
most, ancient sculpture, paintings by the
Old Masters, or the physiognomy of the
people? Something struck me more than
all that [. . .] I want to talk about the
beauty of nature, not only in the country I
now reside, but already in all those that I
traversed since the French border."

## JEAN ALAUX (called LE ROMAIN)
Bordeaux 1785–Paris 1864
*Pensionnaire*, 1816–1820
Director of the Villa Medici, 1847–1852
*François-Édouard Picot in his Studio at
the Villa Medici,* 1817
Oil on canvas, 50.5 x 35.5 cm [19⅞ x 14 in.]
France, Private Collection

ÉMILE JEAN HORACE VERNET
Paris 1789–Paris 1863
  Director of the Villa Medici, 1829–1834
*Portrait of the Artist in his Studio*, 1832
Oil on canvas, 65 x 54.2 cm [25⅝ x 21⅜ in.]
Cleveland Museum of Art

Even though Horace Vernet never won the *prix de Rome*, he became a favorite artist of Louis Philippe, the Duke of Orleans, and many of his Salon paintings were highly praised by the critics. He was elected a member of the French Academy in 1826, and named director of the Villa Medici in 1828. Vernet arrived in Rome with his family in January of the following year.

In Rome, Vernet not only worked hard on his own pictures, but also took his job as director very seriously. In 1829, he wrote to his sister: "My new job as administra-tor is not difficult thanks to the help of Louise [his wife]. I only have the least tedious part of it, but the most delicate one. I assure you, it is not easy to control eighteen self-involved 25 to 35 year-olds. One needs to be firm and very patient. But I do not wish to shake things up and I hope to achieve this (which my predecessors were not able to) without being hated, because up until now the gentlemen *pensionnaires* have only praised me; they do seem to have some affection for me."

ÉMILE JEAN HORACE VERNET
*Louise Vernet*, not dated
Oil on canvas, 100 x 74 cm [39⅜ x 29⅛ in.]
Paris, Musée du Louvre

This quintessentially Romantic portrait represents Louise Vernet, the artist's daughter, with a glimpse of her temporary home in the background. Horace Vernet had brought his wife Louise, their daughter (who bore the same name), and his father, the painter Carle, to live with him in Rome. The charming young Louise was a much appreciated presence in the Villa's predominantly male environment of young, bachelor students. The composer Hector Berlioz wrote that as a *pensionnaire* he enjoyed spending most evenings with Vernet and his family, not least because of the young girl's great beauty. In 1835, Louise Vernet married the painter Paul Delaroche.

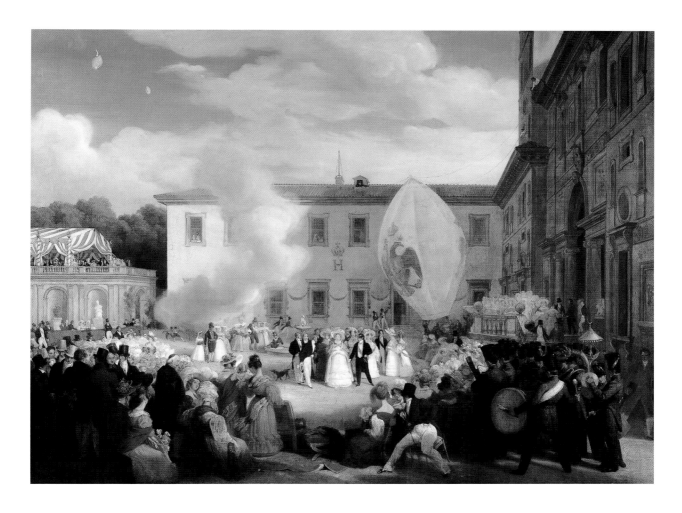

## Louis Dupré

Versailles 1789–Paris 1837
*Chateaubriand Receiving the Grand-Duchess Helen of Russia in the Garden of the Villa Medici, April 29, 1829*
Oil on canvas, 73 x 97 cm [28¾ x 38¼ in.]
Rome, Académie de France

This picture was probably commissioned by the painter Horace Vernet, who had just become director of the Villa Medici at the time of this visit. Dressed in a maroon jacket, he is seen to the left of the guest of honor, while François-René de Chateaubriand stands to the right. Chateaubriand was the ambassador of France in Rome and the host of this elegant party, during which a hot air balloon decorated with the Russian coat of arms was launched.

## Jean Baptiste Joseph Debay

Nantes 1802–Paris 1862
*Pensionnaire, 1830–1834*
*Horace Vernet, 1834*
Director of the Villa Medici, 1829–1834
Marble, 67 x 24.5 x 19.5 cm
[26½ x 9⅝ x 7⅝ in.]
Rome, Académie de France

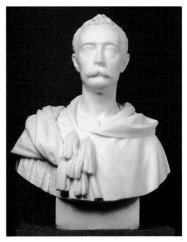

## II.  THE SCHOOL OF ROME: INGRES AND DAVID d'ANGERS

The installation of the French Academy in Rome at the Villa Medici in 1803 marked the re-establishment of the institution, after its suppression in 1792 for being too closely identified with the *ancien régime*, or the French monarchy. Two of the most distinguished artists whose careers signify the consequent rebirth of the "School of Rome" (*l'École de Rome*), as it was called in the 19th century, are the painter Jean Auguste Dominique Ingres (1780–1867) and the sculptor Pierre-Jean David, known as David d'Angers (1788–1856).

The works by Ingres and David d'Angers featured here reveal the entire range of the academic process: from Ingres's *Male Torso* (p. 23), a study of ideal form and proportion conceived at the École des Beaux-Arts in Paris, through the works that were awarded the *prix de Rome* (Ingres's *The Ambassadors of Agamemnon* [p. 25] and David d'Angers's *The Death of Epaminondas* [p. 29]), to the *envoi de Rome*, the work that each artist sent back to Paris every year in order to be judged by the Academy as proof of his artistic development (David d'Angers's, *The Young Herdsman* [p. 25]).

*Copying the Masters*
For artists at the French Academy, copying after the Greek, Roman and Renaissance masters and drawing from the live model played fundamental roles in their professional development. Although this academic exercise was sometimes resented as a necessity, copies by neoclassical painter Hippolyte Flandrin (1809–1864) and the more independent Jean-Baptiste Carpeaux (1827–1875) demonstrate that it enabled students to measure themselves against past masters such as Michelangelo (1475–1564) and Raphael (1483–1520).

Attributed to ERNEST HÉBERT
*Jean Auguste Dominique Ingres*, not dated
Oil on canvas, 46 x 38 cm [18⅛ x 15 in.]
Rome, Académie de France

Attributed to ERNEST HÉBERT
*David d'Angers*, not dated
Oil on canvas, 55 x 46 cm [21¾ x 18⅛ in.]
Rome, Académie de France

## JEAN AUGUSTE DOMINIQUE INGRES

Montauban 1780–Paris 1867
 *Pensionnaire*, 1805–1810
  Director of the Villa Medici, 1835–1840
*Male Torso*, 1800
Oil on canvas, 100 x 80 cm [39¼ x 31½ in.]
Paris, École Nationale Supérieure des Beaux-Arts

Apart from the *prix de Rome* competition, students at the École des Beaux-Arts in Paris competed in other contests. One such category was the *demi-figure peinte*, or painted half figure, for which Ingres won the first prize with this picture in 1800. The purpose of this exercise was to have students paint a torso from a live model within several days. The competitors each took a spot around one model, who was placed in a specific pose (or using the French expression, *mis en attitude*) by the professor. The light source was usually arranged so as to provide the strong dark and light contrast that helped to define the model's body and musculature for the students. The pronounced curve of this figure suggests the early development of Ingres's signature style.

## JEAN-BAPTISTE CARPEAUX

Valenciennes 1827–Courbevoie 1875
 *Pensionnaire*, 1855–1859
*Nude, after Michelangelo*, not dated
Oil on canvas, 72.8 x 51.7 cm
[28⅜ x 20⅜ in.]

Best known as the teacher of Rodin and for his own sculpture *The Dance* on the façade of the Paris Opera, Carpeaux was also active as a painter in Rome. Students at the Villa Medici were required to study the Old Masters, and sculpture students had to send back a copy of an antique statue as one of their *envois de Rome*. The rebellious Carpeaux refused to fulfill this requirement, yet he was deeply affected by the art of Michelangelo. Carpeaux regularly visited the Sistine Chapel in order to try and understand the genius that lay behind Michelangelo's work there.

## PIERRE-JEAN DAVID, called DAVID D'ANGERS

Angers 1788–Paris 1856
*Pensionnaire*, 1812–1815
*The Death of Epaminondas, after the Battle of Mantinea*, 1811
Plaster bas-relief, 111.5 x 159 x 22 cm
[43⅞ x 62⅝ x 8⅝ in.]
Angers, Galerie David d'Angers

In 1811, David d'Angers won the *prix de Rome* for *The Death of Epaminondas*, a work which marked the beginning of a highly successful career. The subject is quite rare and derives from an ancient text by Diodorus of Sicily, the only historian who made mention of this Theban hero's shield being brought to him after he was mortally wounded during battle. The text explains that his friends surrounded the dying warrior and cried out: "Epaminondas, you will die without children! No, he replied, I will leave two daughters, namely the Victory of Leuctra and the Victory of Mantinea. Then he quietly exhaled and they pulled the spear from his wound."

David d'Angers overcame the difficult challenge of visualizing this subject, chosen by the Academy as an *exemplum virtutis* (virtuous example) that was to inspire the viewer to act equally selflessly. In a well-reasoned composition, the artist combined clearly delineated forms, accu-

rate perspective, and convincingly expressed degrees of sorrow. After the death of David d'Anger, the critic Durand wrote of this relief: "It is a page from Plutarch translated with a majestic simplicity and with an ancient and severe elegance."

## DAVID D'ANGERS

Study for *The Death of Epaminondas, after the Battle of Mantinea*, 1811
Graphite on paper, 23.8 x 30.6 cm
[9⅜ x 12 in.]
New York, Dahesh Museum of Art

## JEAN AUGUSTE DOMINIQUE INGRES

Montauban 1780–Paris 1867
  *Pensionnaire*, 1805–1810
  Director of the Villa Medici, 1835–1840
*The Ambassadors of Agamemnon in the Tent of Achilles*, 1801
Oil on canvas, 113 x 146 cm [44½ x 57½ in.]
Paris, École Nationale Supérieure des Beaux-Arts

In 1801, the 21-year old Ingres won the *prix de Rome* with this painting. Taken from the Iliad, it shows the Greek ambassadors Ajax, Phoenix and Ulysses (the three men on the right) pleading with Achilles to resume the battle against Troy. Achilles, seated on the left and accompanied by Patrocles, finishes reciting his verses and stands up in preparation to greet his guests.

The young painter succeeded splendidly in solving the difficulties inherent in rendering such a multi-figure composition, while adhering to the artistic requirements of the Academy. Various ancient works of art have been identified as the compositional sources for individual figures in this painting. Such citations were a basic artistic practice at the time, and neoclassical theory encouraged students to imitate early masterpieces in order to nurture their craft. Ingres was able to retain the sculp-

tural quality of his figures, yet he also managed to animate them with a subtle modeling of flesh tones.

## PIERRE-JEAN DAVID, called DAVID d'ANGERS

Angers 1788–Paris 1856
  *Pensionnaire*, 1812–1815
*The Young Herdsman*, or, *Narcissus*, 1816
Marble, 97 x 46.3 x 43.5 cm [38¼ x 18¼ x 17⅛ in.]
Angers, Galerie David d'Angers

The artist had executed the plaster for this sculpture in 1814. Sculptors were expected to make an exact copy of an ancient sculpture to send back to Paris. David d'Angers deviated from this requirement by creating a study after a young live model in the guise of a classical sculpture.

David d'Angers conceived the subject as a young shepherd mourning a goat he had inadvertently killed with his arrow. Because of some criticism as to the appropriateness of the chosen pose for such a theme, the artist then presented the work as *Narcissus*, the young man who was petrified after seeing his own reflection in the water, and withered away (see also Ernest Hiolle's *Narcissus*, p. 50). That title, however, was eventually abandoned.

## III. THE NUDE AND DRAPERY

A painting like Hippolyte Flandrin's *Polites* (1834) (p. 27) attests to the persistence of the Ingresque classical model in the first half of the 19th century. The works in this section characterize the principal themes of the *envois de Rome*, the paintings or sculptures sent back each year to the Academy in Paris in order to demonstrate their creators' artistic progress. The nude and its necessary ornament, drapery, formed the cornerstones of the academic ideal. The purity, nobility and beauty of the human body–predominantly male–represented the central and single most important element in any history painting.

The representation of the human body as the ultimate academic exercise is here examined throughout the 1840s, showing the stylistic evolution of the assigned themes in both painting and sculpture. The concept could be manifested in a variety of forms: the pastoral (Boissellier, *Shepherd at a Tomb*, 1808; p. 28), the classical god (Blondel, *The Death of Hyacinth*, 1810; p. 29), the virile hero (Foyatier, *Spartacus*, 1824; p. 30), or the more modern incarnation of a popular hero (Barrias, *The Gallic Prisoner*, 1847). On the other hand, religious paintings generally required draped figures (Cabanel, *The Death of Moses*, 1851; p. 31).

**LOUIS-MESSIDOR-LEBON PETITOT**
Paris 1794–Paris 1862
*Pensionnaire, 1815–1819*
*A Young Hunter Wounded by a Serpent*, 1825–1827
Marble, 136 x 95.1 x 50.1 cm
[53½ x 37½ x 19¾ in.]
Paris, Musée du Louvre

The plaster version of this sculpture was made in Rome in 1818 and sent to Paris, where it arrived heavily damaged. After being restored, the work was exhibited at the 1819 Salon, and again at the Salons of 1822 and 1824. Only in 1824 did Petitot receive the commission to execute the marble version depicted here.

Although the young man is supposedly a hunter, symbolized by both his spear and the wolf's skin hanging from his belt, this work has bucolic overtones. Contemporary critics referred to the figure as a shepherd, citing his delicate anatomy and the type of hat he wears.

HIPPOLYTE FLANDRIN
Lyon 1809–Rome 1864
  Pensionnaire, 1833–1837
*Figure Study: Polites, Son of Priam,
Observing the Movements of the Greeks
towards Troy,* 1834
Oil on canvas, 205 x 148 cm
[80¾ x 58¼ in.]
Saint-Étienne, Musée d'Art moderne

Flandrin's first *envoi de Rome* was a figure study drawn from the *Iliad*: "At the moment when the Greek army broke up in order to recommence its attack against Troy, Polites, the youngest son of Priam, was the only one among the Trojans who dared to remain outside the city walls, as he relied on his agility. Seated on the tomb of Oesicles, he observed the movements of the approaching Greeks."

The picture was generally well received for a figure study by a young student. Minor criticism addressed concerns that the model was too individualized and that his hairdo evoked the Middle Ages rather than ancient Greece. Three years later, Flandrin answered such objections with *The Naked Youth* (Paris, Musée du Louvre), depicting a young male nude in profile with his head resting on his knees and facing right.

## Félix Boisselier
Damfal (Haute-Marne) 1776–Rome 1811
*Pensionnaire*, 1807–1810
*A Shepherd Mourning at a Tomb He
Erected to a Gnat*, 1808
Oil on canvas, 195 x 145.5 cm
[76¾ x 57¼ in.]
Palm Beach, Mr. and Mrs. Lee Munder
Collection

Little is known about Félix Boisselier's
life. After he won the *prix de Rome* in
1805, he had to wait one year to go to
Rome, as there was no space available at
the Villa Medici. In Italy he befriended the
painter François-Marius Granet, who
wrote in his diaries about the many painting sessions they enjoyed together in the
countryside. Boisselier's end was
tragic–Granet described his mysterious
disappearance, and a search that ended
with the discovery of Boisselier's body in
the Tiber, a possible suicide. No more
than eight paintings have been recorded
and today only five of them are located.

This picture was Boisselier's second *envoi
de Rome*, based on the *Culex*, a poem
attributed to Virgil during the 19th century. It recounts the story of a shepherd
sleeping near a spring in the woods of the
goddess Diana. When a snake wanted to
drink at the spring, a gnat warned the
shepherd of the pending danger by sting-
ing his eye. Irritated at being woken, the
shepherd crushed the little insect but then
saw the snake and killed it with his staff.
The gnat then appeared in the shepherd's
dream, reproaching his ingratitude. Real-
izing his mistake, the shepherd erected a
tomb to his victim.

**MERRY-JOSEPH BLONDEL**
Paris 1781–Paris 1853
*Pensionnaire*, 1809–1811
*The Death of Hyacinth*, 1810
Oil on canvas, 230 x 151 cm
[90½ x 59½ in.]
Gray, Musée Baron Martin

For his second year *envoi de Rome*, Blondel chose a passage from Ovid about the mortal Hyacinth, whose great beauty incited desire in the gods and who was loved by Apollo. One day, Hyacinth was temporarily blinded by sunlight and killed by the hurtling discus thrown to him by Apollo. Wherever his blood touched the earth, a hyacinth flower grew. Such myths provided artists with the ultimate pretext to render an idealized nude, the core motif of the neoclassical aesthetic.

## DENIS FOYATIER
Bussières (Loire) 1793–Paris 1863
*Spartacus*, 1824
Plaster, 225 x 108 x 71 cm
[88½ x 42½ x 28 in.]
Saint-Étienne, Musée d'Art moderne
[not reproduced]

Never a *prix de Rome* winner, Foyatier lived in Italy on his own accord from 1822 through 1825. He was nonetheless cordially received at the Villa Medici by director Pierre-Narcisse Guérin, and supposedly modeled his *Spartacus* there. In 1827 he exhibited this plaster at the Salon with the following explanation: "Spartacus, the Thracian prince who was enslaved by the Romans, was condemned to perform the vile job of gladiator. Escaping from prison, he gathered some fellow rebels and fought the Romans twice, finally reaching the city walls of Rome [before being slain]. Spartacus is represented at the moment where he breaks his chains and contemplates his vengeance."

Foyatier traveled all the way to Naples to find the perfect model who could personify his concept of Spartacus, but the artist had to settle on a famous Roman athlete. The final pose was found during an angry interchange between artist and model–Foyatier asked him to hold that pose and *Spartacus* was born. The conception of the work was a great challenge to the sculptor, who noted: "After a year of interruption I began working again with courage; but how difficult was it! I wanted to render all at once three episodes from the life of my hero, his slavery, his freedom and his revenge."

*Spartacus* was tremendously popular and was eventually reproduced in many different sizes and materials, most famously in a full-size marble copy for King Charles X (Paris, Musée du Louvre, the work reproduced here). Soon, however, this sculpture came to be seen as a symbol of anti-royalist and even revolutionary and republican ideas. It has also been suggested that *Spartacus* played a role in the public debate about slavery that led to its abolition in France in 1848.

## ALEXANDRE CABANEL

Montpellier 1823–Paris 1889
*Pensionnaire*, 1846–1850
*The Death of Moses*, 1851
Oil on canvas, 284.5 x 304.8 cm
[112 x 120 in.]
New York, Dahesh Museum of Art

Cabanel's last *envoi de Rome* is testimony to his artistic progress and fully embodies his Italian sojourn. The subject, Moses dying before God while being shown the Promised Land that he would never enter, was a daunting enterprise for the 27 year-old artist. He wrote to his brother: "I took upon myself an enormous task, a very difficult and terrifying one, as I seek to render the image of the eternal master of heaven and earth, God in other words, and next to him one of his most sublime creatures who is somehow made divine by his contact. This should give you an idea of my all-absorbing preoccupations. Still, this terrible task advances, but not without cruel mishaps. I know that that's how it is on the path where my instincts have led me, and which is undoubtedly the most beautiful of all the arts, but one has to be strong and love it passionately in order to handle the obstacles one encounters."

Reveling in the masterpieces that surrounded him in Italy, Cabanel was clearly inspired by artists like Michelangelo and Raphael. Following the revolutionary chaos in Rome in 1848, all *pensionnaires* temporarily moved from the Villa Medici to Florence in 1849. There, Cabanel surely encountered Raphael's *The Vision of Ezekiel* (Palazzo Pitti), which, along with Michelangelo's *Creation of Adam* (Rome, Sistine Chapel) were his two main visual sources. In a preliminary drawing (see below) Cabanel contemplated some different compositional solutions, especially in the depiction of God, and also in the angel supporting Moses on the left, who in the painting faces the viewer. At this stage the artist apparently considered but abandoned an arched frame that would have covered the upper corners that are left blank in the drawing.

## ALEXANDRE CABANEL

Study for *The Death of Moses*, ca. 1850
Graphite, pen and brown ink, gray wash, heightened with gouache on paper, 20 x 27.9 cm [7⅞ x 11 in.]
New York, Dahesh Museum of Art

## IV. City and Landscape: Between Myth and Nature

Beyond its great monuments and artistic wealth, the dazzling light and countryside surrounding the Eternal City bewitched every romantic spirit. The French ambassador to Italy, François-René de Chateaubriand, characterized the Roman landscape's beauty as an interchange between natural marvels and epic historical associations. In 1817, the first *prix de Rome* for historical landscape painting was initiated and awarded to Achille-Etna Michallon. This genre is epitomized by Paul Flandrin's *Landscape: The Farewell of an Exile to His Family* (p. 33), which features a majestic natural setting, together with a temple and classical figures added for historical resonance.

The Roman countryside, or the *campagna*, was also used by artists for painting directly from life. Since the beginning of the 19th century, history painters such as Guillaume Bodinier, Joseph-Désiré Court and Charles-Philippe Larivière made outings together to paint the distinctive light of the Italian countryside *en plein air* (in open air).

Within the walls of Rome, of course, distinguished ancient sites such as the Colosseum and Forum Romanum also inspired a great number of artists, both for their picturesque and historical significance. The Vatican and countless churches, convents and monasteries formed another primary motif, underlining Rome's centrality within the Catholic faith, in which most French artists of the time were raised.

PAUL FLANDRIN
Lyon 1811–Paris 1902
*A Herd of Steers in the Roman Campagna*, 1835
Oil on canvas, 55 x 82 cm [21⅝ x 32¼ in.]
Paris, Private Collection

This painting gives a good impression of the expansive countryside near Rome that attracted so many artists. Flandrin wrote in 1834 to one of his friends: "I'm not surprised that you have talked to me so often about the Roman countryside. It's sublime! What character! And then those herds of bulls in the distance, with these horseback riders who guide them, all that really has character and that can only be found there."

PAUL FLANDRIN
Lyon 1811–Paris 1902
*Landscape: The Farewell of an Exile to His Family*, or, *The Sabine Mountains*, 1838
Oil on canvas, 201 x 150 cm [79⅛ x 59 in.]
Paris, Musée du Louvre

Paul Flandrin stayed in Rome from 1834 through 1838, and debuted at the Paris Salon of 1839 with this impressive landscape. Even though he did not win the *prix de Rome*, he followed his brother Hippolyte, who was *pensionnaire* at the Villa Medici from 1833 through 1837. This picture is clearly informed by his Italian experience as well as by the historical landscape tradition. With the addition of a viaduct, a temple and classically dressed figures, the work clearly fell within the official landscape category accepted by the Academy.

When Flandrin exhibited the work again at the Salon of 1852, he renamed it *Montagnes de la Sabine*. This not only reflects the rule that a picture could not be exhibited more than once under the same title, but also may reflect a changing attitude towards the genre of historical landscape painting (the *prix de Rome* for historical landscape painting was abandoned in 1863). The later title stresses the work's Italian connection, depicting mountains near Rome, rather than a scene from classical history.

**FRANÇOIS-MARIUS GRANET**
Aix-en-Provence 1775–Aix-en-Provence
1849
*View of the Interior of the Colosseum,*
1804
Oil on canvas, 125 x 160 cm [49¼ x 63 in.]
Paris, Musée du Louvre

The Colosseum was one of Granet's
favorite Roman buildings. This painting
dates from his early stay in the city, and
records the building before its restoration
by Napoleon between 1808 and 1814.
The artist wrote: "I have decided to do
some studies from nature. I chose the
Colosseum. This building is so beautiful in
its remarkable form and the vegetation
that envelopes its ruins, and it produces
such an enchanting effect under the sky."
Granet transformed this impressive view
of the monument into a genre scene with
local people praying before a crucifix, a
reminder that Christianity had conquered
pagan Rome.

**FRANÇOIS-MARIUS GRANET**
*At the Colosseum, A Painter at Work,*
not dated
Oil on canvas, 28.5 x 22.5 cm [11¼ x 8⅞ in.]
Private Collection

This charming little sketch of a painter at
work in the ruins of the Colosseum could
easily have illustrated an informative letter
Granet wrote to another painter in 1836,
six years after he left Rome: *My dear
friend, I'm happy you will be in Rome.
You will be in a beautiful land that you
will have to carefully observe while you're
there. You ask my advice of what to do,
and here are my thoughts: first, work
every day and never come home without
having something to put into your portfo-
lio, even on those days when you try
painting from nature. As the effect of
what you are studying won't last all day
[due to changing light effects], there will
always be time to make a drawing. At the
end, you will have your picture finished
and also as many drawings as it took days
to finish it. I don't think you will be able
to make finished drawings, but you can
always make outlines with good indica-
tions of color values, so once you are
home you can fill in tones with ink or
bistre while your memory is still fresh.
Make sure that the tone values are well
observed. When all that is done, guard all
these scraps of paper well until you've
returned to Paris, there you can choose the
best among them.*

JEAN BAPTISTE CAMILLE
COROT
Paris 1796–Paris 1875
*Rome: View Taken from the Window of
the Artist*, 1825
Oil on paper, adhered to panel, 14.5 x
23.1 cm [5¾ x 9⅛ in.]
Paris, Private Collection

Corot never competed for the *prix de
Rome*, but traveled to Italy at his own
expense. He had already painted outdoors
in Paris and Fontainebleau, but he really
matured as a landscape painter in Italy.
When he arrived in Rome in December
1825, he rented a room on the fourth
floor of the Palazzo dei Pupazzi, near the
Spanish Steps and the Villa Medici. Corot

evidently took the advice of his influential
mentor Pierre Henri de Valenciennes, who
wrote: "Paint after nature, even after a
rain shower, because you must see something from your window, paint no matter
what." This touching little sketch represents a point of departure for Corot, in
whose prolific career the Italian landscape
would play a central role.

GUILLAUME BODINIER
Paris 1795–Angers 1872
*Panorama of Rome seen from the Gardens
of Mount Pincio*, 1824
Oil on paper, adhered to cardboard,
17.5 x 29.5 cm [6⅞ x 11⅝ in.]
Angers, Musée des Beaux-Arts

Although not a *prix de Rome* winner,
Bodinier followed his teacher Pierre-Narcisse Guérin to Rome in 1822 when the
latter became the director at the Villa
Medici. Bodinier stayed in Italy until
1847, making only brief visits to France.
The artist made numerous excursions in
the city as well as into the countryside to
study the varied Italian landscape. Thus
he created a great number of sketches like
this view over Rome. Their informal
brushwork contrasts greatly with the
highly finished style of his large Salon
painting of 1825, *The Marriage Proposal.
Costumes of Albano, near Rome* (p. 41), a
work that nonetheless reveals a similar
interest in the exotic qualities of Italy.

FRANÇOIS-ÉDOUARD BERTIN
Paris 1797–Paris 1871
*View of the Quarries of Cervara, near
Rome*, 1839
Oil on canvas, 180 x 150 cm
[70⅞ x 59 in.]
Carcassonne, Musée des Beaux-Arts

The Cervara quarries south of Rome form
an arid and wild landscape with beautiful
cliffs tinged in ochre and red. Foreign
artists, including Camille Corot, frequently painted this picturesque area. Bertin
submitted this imposing landscape as a
"souvenir" to the 1839 Paris Salon. This
term was often used in the title of a painting when the artist had actually visited the
region. In fact, paintings of this format
were actually painted in the artist's studio,
working from drawings and sketches.

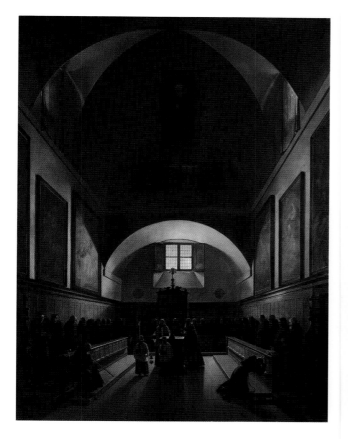

## FRANÇOIS-MARIUS GRANET
Aix-en-Provence 1775–Aix-en-Provence
1849
*The Choir of the Capuchin Church in Rome*, 1815
Oil on canvas, 196.9 x 148 cm [77½ x 58¼ in.]
New York, The Metropolitan Museum of Art, Gift of L.P. Everard, 1880. (80.5.2)
Photograph © 1980 The Metropolitan Museum of Art

This painting is probably the first of at least sixteen versions of the composition that Granet painted between 1814 and 1822. It represents the choir, or private chapel, of Santa Maria della Concezione, the church of the Capuchin friary on the Piazza Barberini in Rome. It is believed that the scene represents the "Asperges," the solemn blessing with holy water that preceded the Sunday High Mass. The painting became immensely popular from the moment that Caroline Murat, Napoleon's sister, saw it in Granet's Roman studio around 1815. Latin sonnets were written in praise of it, Pope Pius VII

admired it, and the King of Spain and Lord Cunningham ordered smaller copies. Granet exhibited a large replica in the Salon of 1819; that version won him the Legion of Honor and was probably bought by the Duchess of Berry. Granet's subtle handling of light, the atmosphere of calm devotion, and much-admired realism help account for the picture's immense appeal. In addition, the intimate piety of cloistered ritual conformed to the spirit of the Roman Catholic revival during the French restoration of the monarchy in 1815.

## JEAN AUGUSTE DOMINIQUE INGRES
Montauban 1780–Paris 1867
*Pensionnaire*, 1805–1810
Director of the Villa Medici, 1835–1840
*Pope Pius VII in the Sistine Chapel*, 1814
Oil on canvas, 74.5 x 92.7 cm [29⅜ x 36½ in.]
Washington DC, National Gallery of Art

This image of Pope Pius VII celebrating High Mass in the Sistine Chapel (Michel-

angelo's *Last Judgment* is visible at the right) suggests an eyewitness account, as Ingres depicted himself among the brown-clad train-bearers, fourth from the left. Yet, Pius VII—who had crowned Napoleon emperor—could not have been leading this ceremony in 1814, as he was being held prisoner in France after his forcible removal from Rome following Napoleon's annexation of the Papal States in 1809.

Ingres was commissioned to paint the picture by his good friend and patron Charles Marcotte, a prominent French official in Rome. Marcotte might have been expected to avoid such a potentially controversial commission. Indeed, the painting was not exhibited in Paris until the political situation had changed dramatically. Napoleon's defeat and exile and the return of King Louis XVIII in 1815, as well as the pope's own restoration to Rome removed whatever controversy clung to Marcotte's commission.

# V. THE ROMAN PEOPLE: FROM THE HEROIC TO THE PICTURESQUE

Many intellectuals including Chateaubriand and Stendhal adhered to the myth of the Roman people as the uncorrupted inheritors of ideal classical beauty—as modern incarnations of ancient heroes. Likewise, artists such as Théodore Géricault, Léopold Robert, Horace Vernet and Victor Schnetz cultivated a visual mythology of both the common people and brigands, who were believed to lead free and unencumbered lives. Resident artists at the Villa Medici, as well as artist-visitors like Théodore Chassériau and Edgar Degas, contributed to this myth by depicting the savage nobility of local men and the graceful dignity of women.

ACHILLE-ETNA MICHALLON
Paris 1796–Paris 1822
*Pensionnaire*, 1818–1821
*Mazzochi, an Italian Brigand*, not dated
Oil on canvas, 35 x 27 cm [13¾ x 10⅝ in.]
Orléans, Musée des Beaux-Arts

This portrait of the brigand Mazzochi, "famous for his beauty, his dexterity and his exploits," is a fine example of the popular genre of brigand scenes. The narrative context of this painting was added in the studio. The work is based on one of several studies of Mazzochi in exactly the same pose.

Normally encountered outside of Rome, brigands experienced a severe crackdown in 1819, and many were imprisoned within the city. A year later, the director of the Villa Medici, Charles Thévenin, requested a permit allowing Michallon to paint and draw "in the prisons of Termini, where the inhabitants of the surroundings of Rome are detained." According to Thévenin, the prison population served as a source for many types: "[as] one finds together the diverse costumes of peasant women which are very interesting for landscape painters because of their variety or singularity, and they are a necessary part of the studies for which they come to Italy."

ÉMILE JEAN HORACE VERNET
Paris 1789–Paris 1863
  Director of the Villa Medici, 1829–1834
*The Confession of a Brigand*, 1831
Oil on canvas, 150 x 230 cm [59 x 90½ in.]
Paris, Private Collection

This picture, together with *Italian Brigands Surprised by the Papal Troops* (Baltimore, The Walters Art Museum) was among the 12 paintings shown by Vernet at the Salon of 1831. Several works in this group had been inspired by the artist's new surroundings in Rome. King Louis Philippe of France started his reign in 1831 and counted Vernet among his favorite painters. When the artist returned to France, the King commissioned several history paintings from him for the historical galleries at Versailles.

JEAN-VICTOR SCHNETZ
Versailles 1787–Paris 1870
  Director of the Villa Medici, 1841–1846
  and 1853–1865
*The Fortune-teller*, not dated
Oil on canvas, 74.5 x 62.3 cm
[29⅜ x 24½ in.]
Clermont-Ferrand, Musée d'art Roger-
Quillot

Schnetz tried several times without success
to win the *prix de Rome*, before he
reached the age of 30 and could no longer
enter the competition. Undaunted, he
traveled to Italy on his own in 1816, and
many years later became director of the
Villa Medici for two terms. Like François-
Joseph Navez and Léopold Robert,
Schnetz often painted peasants from the
environs of Rome. The woman posing for
the fortune-teller in this painting is the
same model who appears in at least four
more contemporaneous pictures.

THÉODORE GÉRICAULT
Rouen 1791–Paris 1824
*The Old Italian Woman*, not dated
Oil on canvas, 62 x 50 cm [24⅜ x 19⅝ in.]
Le Havre, Musée Malraux

The attribution of this painting has only
recently changed from Schnetz to Géricault. It shows the same model as in
Schnetz's *The Fortune-teller*. However,
some scholars retain the authorship of
Schnetz, while others give it to François-
Joseph Navez. Géricault was in Italy for
only one year, beginning in the autumn of
1816.

## GUILLAUME BODINIER
Paris 1795–Angers 1872
*The Marriage Proposal. Costumes of
Albano, near Rome,* 1825
Oil on canvas, 98 x 135 cm [38½ x 53⅛ in.]
Angers, Musée des Beaux-Arts

Although not a *prix de Rome* winner,
Bodinier followed his teacher Pierre-Narcisse Guérin in 1822 when the latter
became the director at the Villa Medici.
Bodinier stayed in Italy until 1847, making only brief visits to France. For his first
Salon in 1827, he submitted this genre
painting of a man asking a mother for the
hand of her daughter. The description
"Costumes of Albano," from the Salon
catalogue, testifies to the artist's interest in
rural Italian communities and their exotic
costumes.

## JULES LENEPVEU
Angers 1819–Paris 1898
 *Pensionnaire,* 1848–1852
 Director of the Villa Medici, 1873–1878
*Study of an Italian Model*
Oil on canvas, 50 x37 cm [19¹¹⁄₁₆ x 14⁹⁄₁₆ in.]
Maine, Private Collection, photogaph
courtesy W. M. Brady & Co., Inc.

This study must have been painted during
Lenepveu's years as a *pensionnaire* at the
Villa Medici. Jean-Léon Gérôme had
already painted this model's strikingly
expressive face during his Roman trip in
1844, and about a decade later Edgar
Degas also drew him in various poses.

JEAN-BAPTISTE CARPEAUX
Valenciennes 1827–Courbevoie 1875
 *Pensionnaire*, 1855–1859
*Two Studies of a Young Woman from
Trastevere*, 1858
Oil on canvas, 40.3 x 32.5 cm
[15⅞ x 12¾ in.]
Valenciennes, Musée des Beaux-Arts

Trastevere was a popular neighborhood
on the right bank of the Tiber, where
artists easily found models willing to pose.
While this sketch may have been taken
from a live model, it betrays the hand of a
sculptor, primarily interested in the monumental qualities of his subject seen from
two slightly different angles.

JEAN-BAPTISTE CARPEAUX
*Palombella Wearing a 'Panno,'* 1860s
Terracotta, 68.5 x 50 x 32 cm
[27 x 19⅝ x 12⅝ in.]
Valenciennes, Musée des Beaux-Arts

Carpeaux was infatuated with Barbara
Pasquarelli, a young orphan girl from the
village of Palomabarra, near Rome. He
wanted to marry her, but the rules of the
Villa Medici prevented *pensionnaires* from
marrying. In 1861, Barbara married a
shepherd and died later that year.
Carpeaux made one sculpture of her in
1860, and after her death continued to use
her face in various sculptures. Here she
wears a traditional headdress, a *panno*,
which is Italian for cloth.

## ÉMILE JEAN HORACE VERNET
Paris 1789–Paris 1863
  Director of the Villa Medici, 1829–1834
*The Start of the Race of Riderless Horses,*
ca. 1820
Oil on canvas, 46 x 54 cm [18⅛ x 21¼ in.]
New York, The Metropolitan Museum of
Art, Catharine Lorillard Wolfe Collection,
Bequest of Catharine Lorillard Wolfe,
1887. (87.15.47) Photograph © 1994 The
Metropolitan Museum of Art

The riderless horse race, the most exciting
event of the Roman carnival, captivated
artists and writers, among them Géricault
and Goethe. This is a sketch for a larger
painting of 1820 (private collection). It
depicts the dramatic start of the mile-and-
a-half race along the length of the Via del
Corso in Rome, from Piazza del Popolo to
Piazza Venezia. Just before the race
begins, grooms strained to control the
small, half-wild Barberi horses, who were
roused both by the cheering crowds and
the spurs pressed in their sides. Vernet
witnessed this event during his first trip to
Rome, and he is said to have included
other French painters then in the city
among the spectators in the stands.

# VI. FROM INGRES'S CLASSICISM TO THE TRIUMPH OF ECLECTICISM

Ingres's term as director of the French Academy in Rome (1835–1840) introduced an era of remarkable stylistic coherence that stressed the nobility of history and the purity of line. While all academic art—encompassing religious, mythological and historical themes—was subjugated to the rigor of contour and line, it could nonetheless convey a degree of sensuality (Bouguereau, *The Battle between the Centaurs and the Lapiths*, 1852; p. 52) or lend itself to charming *néo-grec* evocations (Perraud, *The Farewell of Jason*, 1848–49; p. 48).

Around 1850, by which time academic painting had assumed an established rhetoric, artists began exploring new subjects and modes of expression. The following two decades—marked by the 1863 teaching reforms at the École des Beaux-Arts as well as by the *Salon des Refusés*—saw the break from the Ingresque norm. A number of painters and sculptors pursued alternative points of view while staying loyal to academic traditions (Merson, *Saint Edmond, King of England, Martyr*, 1871; p. 51). These artists occupy a significant place in the history of art and herald other avenues of expression, including Symbolism.

**JEAN AUGUSTE DOMINIQUE INGRES**
Montauban 1780–Paris 1867
*Pensionnaire*, 1805–1810
Director of the Villa Medici, 1835–1840
*Antiochus and Stratonice*, or, *The Illness of Antiochus*, ca. 1858–60
Oil on canvas, 35 x 45 cm [13¾ x 17¾ in.]
Private Collection, courtesy Philadelphia Museum of Art

Before leaving for Rome in 1834 to become the director of the Villa Medici, Ingres received a commission from the Duke of Orleans, the son of King Louis Philippe, to make a pendant for the painting by Paul Delaroche, *The Death of the Duke of Guise* (Chantilly, Musée Condé). The subject agreed upon was the illness of the Syrian king Antiochus. Ingres struggled with this subject, writing in 1837: "Even though I work very hard, I still have not finished my grand historical miniature." In 1840 he finally completed the work (Chantilly, Musée Condé) and it was well received. Ingres painted this smaller version in 1858–60.

Antiochus was passionately in love with Stratonice, queen of upper Asia and the wife of his father Seleucus. Aware that his desires were unlawful but too strong to resist, he preferred to die by starvation. His doctor Erasistratus perceived that love was his real illness and wanted to identify the object of his affection. The doctor watched his patient closely when various court beauties came to visit, and saw at once that only Stratonice produced an emotional reaction.

(not included in the exhibition)

**JEAN LOUIS NICOLAS JALEY**
Paris 1802–Neuilly-sur-Seine 1866
 *Pensionnaire*, 1828–1832
*Modesty*, 1833
Marble, 116 x 47 x 37 cm
[45⅝ x 18½ x 14⅝ in.]
Paris, Musée du Louvre

As his last *envoi de Rome* in 1832, Jaley executed in plaster a half-nude female figure entitled *Modesty*. He exhibited this marble version at the Salon of 1834. The image of a young girl covering herself follows on a long iconographic tradition of Venus surprised at her bath. It is not known whether the narrow width of this sculpture was dictated by the block of marble, yet Jaley managed to create a graceful pose that provides two very distinctive three-quarter frontal views.

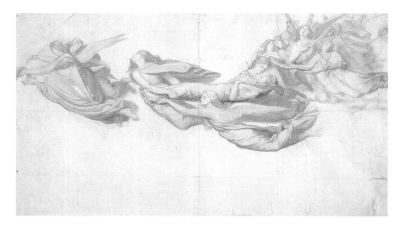

## HENRI LEHMANN
Kiel 1814–Paris 1882
*Saint Catherine of Alexandria Carried to Her Tomb*, 1839
Oil on canvas, 152 x 262 cm
[59⅞ x 103⅛ in.]
Montpellier, Musée Fabre

As a German, Lehmann was ineligible to compete for the *prix de Rome*, even though he lived and studied in Paris. In 1838, however, he followed his former teacher Ingres, who had become the director of the French Academy in Rome, and frequented the cultural evenings organized at the Villa Medici. In addition to his famous portrait of composer Franz Liszt (1839, Paris, Musée Carnavalet), Lehmann sent to the 1840 Paris Salon *St. Catherine of Alexandria Carried to Her Tomb*, for which he received a first-class medal. This work reveals not only a debt to Ingres but also a fascination with the Italian primitives and Lehmann's fellow German Nazarenes, who worked in Italy as well.

Three angels carry the body of St. Catherine to Mount Sinai, while another group sings and plays music. Three more angels lead the way bearing remnants of one of the spiked wheels on which the Emperor Maxentius martyred Catherine in the early fourth century. The striking two-dimensional effect that Lehmann achieved by setting his figures against the symbolic space of the sky, and with the Fra Angelico-inspired faces of the angels, clearly evoke the early Renaissance aesthetic that so many contemporary artists and patrons wished to revive.

## HENRI LEHMANN
Study for *Saint Catherine of Alexandria Carried to Her Tomb*, ca. 1839
Graphite on paper, 50.8 x 88.8 cm
[20 x 35 in.]
New York, Dahesh Museum of Art, Gift of DeCourcy E. McIntosh

**JULES-ÉLIE DELAUNAY**
Nantes 1828–Paris 1891
*Pensionnaire, 1857–1860*
*The Communion of the Apostles,* 1861
Oil on canvas, 280 x 202 cm
[110¼ x 79½ in.]
Nantes, Musée des Beaux-Arts

In this scene depicting the Last Supper, Christ offers bread to the apostles Peter and John. Delaunay created this work in his last year in Rome, after the bishop of Nantes had asked him to paint an altarpiece for the cathedral of his native town. Clearly inspired by artists such as Raphael and Poussin, Delaunay placed the three main figures in a triangle, while the remaining apostles recede in more muted tones into the background. Once the picture had arrived in France, however, the work appeared too dark for its allotted space, and Delaunay created a second, brighter version that took its place.

## JEAN JOSEPH PERRAUD
Monay 1819–Paris 1876
*Pensionnaire*, 1848–1852
*The Farewell of Jason*, 1848–49
Plaster bas-relief, 197 x 182 x 24.5 cm
[77½ x 71⅝ x 9⅝ in.]
Lons-le-Saunier, Musée des Beaux-Arts

This rarely depicted subject shows Jason bidding farewell to his parents Aeson and Alkimede, before leaving with the Argonauts to capture the Golden Fleece. This emotional event occurs under the watchful trio of statuettes in the upper right corner, representing the deities Juno, Neptune and Minerva.

Sent as Perraud's first *envoi de Rome*, this plaster arrived heavily damaged in Paris, due to the revolutionary unrest there in 1848. The French State acquired it in 1871, and commissioned a marble version the following year. The pencil markings visible on the plaster relate to the technique used to duplicate it.

**EUGÈNE GUILLAUME**
Montbard (Côte-d'or) 1822–Rome 1905
 *Pensionnaire*, 1846–1850
  Director of the Villa Medici, 1891–1896
*The Cenotaph of the Gracchi*, 1880
Marble, 84 x 82 x 40 cm
[33⅟₁₆ x 32⁵⁄₁₆ x 15¾ in.]
Collection of Mr. Max Blumberg and Mr.
Carlos Eduardo Araujo

For Guillaume's first *envoi de Rome* in 1848, the artist had to create "a head study expressing a subject." A plaster sculpture of the present composition was sent back to Paris. Guillaume exhibited a bronze version at the 1853 Salon (Paris, Musée d'Orsay), and much later in life he carved this marble. The Latin inscription reads: "To the Gracchi, Tiberius and

Caius Sempronius, tribunes of the plebe, who gave to the Roman people the greatest services." Although no actual funerary monument to the Gracchi is known, Guillaume was certainly inspired by related examples he would have seen in Rome.

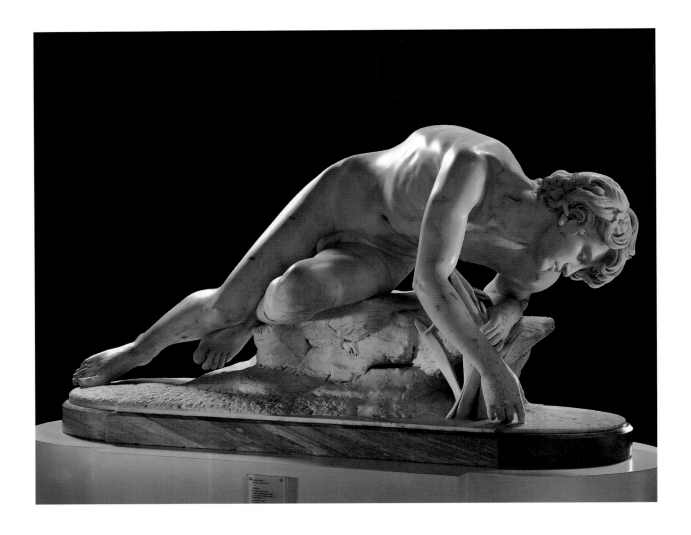

ERNEST HIOLLE
Paris 1834–Bois-le-Roi 1886
 *Pensionnaire*, 1863–1867
*Narcissus*, 1868
Marble, 87 x 160 x 64 cm [34¼ x 63
x 25¼ in.]
Valenciennes, Musée des Beaux-Arts

For his last *envoi de Rome*, Hiolle was
inspired by the tragic story of Narcissus in
Ovid's *Metamorphoses*. This handsome
adolescent, who disdainfully rejected the
advances of numerous nymphs, was punished by the vengeful goddess Nemesis.
She made him fall in love with his own
reflection while drinking from a pond.
"Paralyzed by this image so similar to his
own, he remained petrified, like a sculpture in marble of Paros." His suffering
and subsequent death moved the gods and
transformed him into the little flower that
bears his name.

## LUC-OLIVIER MERSON
Paris 1846–Paris 1920
*Pensionnaire*, 1870–1873
*Saint-Edmond, King of England, Martyr*,
1871
Oil on canvas, 145.5 x 226 cm [57¼ x 89 in.]
Troyes, Musée des Beaux-Arts

This subject from medieval British history is a great anomaly for a painting made as an *envoi de Rome* at the Villa Medici. The

1872 Salon catalogue explained the subject as follows: "In 870, Inwar, King of Denmark, invaded England and captured its King Edmond. He attached him to a tree, and after his body was pierced with arrows, he decapitated him." According to legend, a wolf guarded the King's head until his body was found again, explaining the ferocious animal seen here next to the *putto* holding the royal arms and a palm symbolizing martyrdom.

This was Merson's first large-scale religious painting, a genre he was eager to revive, partly due to the influence of his father, a painter, critic and great champion of religious painting. Merson's stylized rendition of Edmond's martyrdom could be called proto-symbolist; while the weapons of execution are placed next to his lifeless body, the body itself is unblemished and the bloodshed is suggested only by a piece of red fabric.

ADOLPHE-WILLIAM
BOUGUEREAU
La Rochelle 1825–La Rochelle 1905
  *Pensionnaire*, 1851–1853
*The Battle between the Centaurs and the
Lapiths*, 1852
Oil on canvas, 123 x 174 cm [48½ x 68½ in.]
Private Collection

The Centaurs and the Lapiths were neigh-
boring tribes in ancient Thessaly in north-
eastern Greece, with a long history of
conflict. As a peace offering, Pirithoos,
King of the Lapiths, invited a number of
Centaurs to his wedding to Hippodamia.
After the Centaur Eurytion drank too
much wine at the celebration, he tried to

abduct the bride. He was pursued down
and punished, and, after a full-scale battle,
the Centaurs were expelled from Thessaly.

The battle between these feuding parties
was a recurring theme in Greek art.
Although a young student, Bouguereau
did not shy away from this complicated
visual motif. In homage to classical sculpture, he devised a composition that features frieze-like groupings in three planes,
focusing on the abduction of Hippodamia
and on Pirithoos's attempt to rescue her.
Bouguereau invested great effort in rendering the elaborate drapery–a key com-
ponent of academic training–that
envelopes the figure of Hippodamia.

**JOSEPH-PAUL BLANC**
Paris 1846–Paris 1904
 *Pensionnaire*, 1868–1871
*Perseus*, 1869
Oil on canvas, 299 x 175 cm
[117¾ x 68⅞ in.]
Nîmes, Musée des Beaux-Arts

Perseus, the son of Danaë, had been assigned the seemingly impossible task of retrieving the horrific head of the Gorgon, Medusa. Medusa was once a beautiful maiden, but Poseidon ravished her in the shrine of Athena, who changed her countenance to that of a nightmarish demon with snakes growing from her head and the power to turn men to stone. Averting his gaze from Medusa, Perseus severed the head from her slumbering body and made his escape on the winged Pegasus.

For his first *envoi de Rome*, the 23-year-old Blanc was required to realize "a life-size figure painted after nature." This fervent image suggests the student's unbridled ambition to become a great history painter, and the ingenious modeling of the hero's body shows Blanc's mastery of this academic assignment. After *Perseus* was exhibited at the 1870 Salon, the government acquired it for the Musée du Luxembourg, then the national museum of French contemporary art. After the 1880s, however, the demand for history painting diminished significantly, and Blanc and many of his colleagues worked primarily on decorative schemes for government buildings.

**EDGAR HILAIRE GERMAIN DEGAS**
Paris 1834–Paris 1917
*Dante and Virgil at the Entrance to the Inferno*, 1857–1858
Oil on canvas, 111.5 x 75.5 cm
[44 x 29¾ in.]
Private Collection, courtesy Haggerty Museum of Art, Marquette University, Milwaukee

Painted in Rome, this is one of Degas's first major compositions and illustrates three stanzas of Canto II from Dante's *Inferno*. It shows Virgil taking Dante by the hand as he reads an inscription over the gate of hell:

*Through me is the way into the doleful city;*
*through me the way into the eternal pain;*
*through me the way among the people lost.*

*Justice moved my High Maker;*
*Divine Power made me,*
*Wisdom Supreme, and Primal Love.*

*Before me were no things created, but eternal;*
*and eternal I endure:*
*leave all hope, ye that enter.*

The young Degas stood at the beginning of his career when he created this picture and was full of self-doubt. In Italy he had befriended Gustave Moreau, who men-tored him, and his father wrote encouragingly after receiving some paintings from Rome: "I was very pleased and I can tell you that you have made immense strides in your art; your draughtmanship is very strong, your color tones are right [. . . ]. You have a fine destiny before you, don't be discouraged, don't trouble your mind."

Apart from the clear influence of Delacroix upon this painting, the model for the figure of Dante may have been the engraver Joseph-Gabriel Tourny (1817–1880), who befriended Degas in Rome. According to annotations on a preparatory study, the figure of Virgil is based upon that of the Virgin Mary by Fra Angelico.

PIERRE JULES CAVELIER
Paris 1814–Paris 1898
  *Pensionnaire*, 1843–1847
*Tragedy*, 1854
Plaster, 86 cm high [33⅞ in.]
New York, Dahesh Museum of Art

In 1845, Cavelier sent as his second *envoi de Rome* a study of a head (*tête d'étude*) called *Tragedy*. Ten years later, at the 1855 Universal Exhibition in Paris, he exhibited a bronze (location unknown) with the same title, which probably resembled his earlier *envoi*. This plaster is inscribed "1854" and thus relates to the creation of the bronze.

The title of this work alludes not only to the figure's stern downward gaze but also to the theatrical mask of Tragedy that rests on the back of the head. Ancient Greek actors wore such masks attached with ribbons that allowed them to place the mask on their face or on top of their head. The relationship of this mask's tragic expression to the petrifying gaze of Medusa is conveyed by the snake that curls in the form of a necklace.

## VII. BEYOND ROME: CLASSICISM OF THE IMAGINATION

This exhibition concludes with several paintings that evoke the continued influence that the Roman sojourn exerted upon French artists, even after they returned home. Whether *pensionnaires* at the Villa Medici or not, artists who had spent a significant period in Italy all found something to cherish in this land of cultural and natural riches. This classicism of the imagination was nurtured by memories and associations of their experience.

Jules-Élie Delaunay's morbid *The Plague in Rome* cites several well-known monuments from the Eternal City and also emulates the Old Master paintings he had encountered there. Gustave Moreau's *Hesiod and the Muses* illustrates a passage from classical literature and takes its subdued coloring from ancient frescoes. And Pierre Puvis de Chavannes's *Young Women at the Seashore* with its stylized figures in classical poses contains a hint of abstraction that paved the way for a modernist aesthetic that would ultimately prevail.

ERNEST HÉBERT
Grenoble 1817–La Tronche (Isère) 1908
  *Pensionnaire*, 1840-44
  Director of the Villa Medici, 1867–1872
*Malaria*, 1848–49
Oil on canvas, 135 x 193 cm [53⅛ x 76 in.]
Paris, Musée d'Orsay

This poignant rendering of Italian peasants crossing the Pontine marshes on a barge was painted in Hébert's studio in Paris, five years after he left Italy. Malaria, "bad air" in Italian, was a constant worry in the region of Latium and Rome and regularly discussed in 19th-century Italian travel literature. In 1826, William Hazlitt wrote in his *English Students at Rome*: "there is a species of *malaria* hanging over it, which infects both the mind and the body . . . There is languor in the air; and the contagion of listless apathy infects the hopes that are yet unborn."

The critic Théophile Gautier thought Hébert's picture "presented an original and true Italy; the picturesque is unified with sentiment. There are no longer these bronzed types, nicely rendered in a bright light, but an unwholesome grace, a nervous melancholy, a sad poetry that touches my heart."

JULES-ÉLIE DELAUNAY
Nantes 1828–Paris 1891
*Pensionnaire* from 1857–1860
*The Plague in Rome*, 1869
Oil on canvas, 131 x 176.5 cm
[51⅛ x 79½ in.]
Paris, Musée d'Orsay

This picture depicts a scene from the life of Saint Sebastian as recounted in the *Golden Legend* by Jacopo de Voragine (13th century): "And thus appeared a good angel who ordered a bad angel carrying a spear to knock on the door as many times as deaths would occur in that house." After having visited the church of San Pietro in Vincoli, Delaunay was inspired by a picture commemorating the pestilence that had devastated Rome in 1476. His first sketch of this subject dates from 1857; two years later he sent an *envoi de Rome* with the same theme. In Paris, he conceived this striking painting, exhibited at the Salon of 1869. It contains numerous references to Delaunay's stay in Rome, including the equestrian statue of Marcus Aurelius, the tower of the Milizie, the staircase of the Santa Maria de l'Aracoeli, and the silhouette of the Palace of the Conservatori.

## GUSTAVE MOREAU
Paris 1826–Paris 1898
*Hesiod and the Muses*, ca. 1860
Oil on canvas, 133 x 133 cm [52⅜ x 52⅜ in.]
Paris, Musée Gustave Moreau

Having failed to win the *prix de Rome* competition in 1848 and 1849, Moreau abandoned his studies at the École des Beaux-Arts in Paris. He eventually traveled to Rome in 1857, where he studied the Renaissance masters and attended drawing classes with live models at the Villa Medici. Moreau visited other Italian cities and met Degas, who became a close friend, before returning to France in 1859.

Hesiod, a Greek poet of the seventh century B.C., wrote the *Theogony*, a book Moreau knew from childhood. While in Italy, Moreau made various drawings of the subject that he used to create the present painting. It was inspired by the opening lines of the *Theogony*, in which the muses reveal the divine mysteries to the shepherd-poet, shown here wearing a pointed cap, and then crown him in the presence of the sacred swan of Apollo. The gestures of Hesiod and the kneeling muse may have been inspired by the central group of Perugino's *Christ Delivering the Keys to Saint Peter* in the Sistine Chapel. The monochromatic quality of

this picture points to the Pompeian frescoes that Moreau copied during his Italian travels.

## Edgar Hilaire Germain Degas

Paris 1834–Paris 1917
*Woman on a Terrace*, or *Young Woman and Ibis*, 1857–58, reworked ca. 1860–62
Oil on canvas, 98 x 74 cm [38⅝ 29⅛ in.]
Private Collection

During Degas's second stay in Rome, between October 1857 and July 1858, he made several preparatory drawings for this painting. Degas originally intended the work to be a variant of a composition by Hippolyte Flandrin entitled *Dreaming* (location unknown). It too shows a woman in a pensive mode, reminiscent of the figure in Ingres's *Antiochus and Stratonice* (p. 44). Upon his return to Paris in the early 1860s, Degas altered the painting's conception by adding both the pseudo-Oriental city in the background and the red ibis. This gradual change–from a mostly classical composition into a more exotic one–may have occurred under the influence of Gustave Moreau.

PIERRE PUVIS DE CHAVANNES
Lyon 1824–Paris 1898
*Young Women at the Seashore*, 1881
Oil on canvas, 61 x 47 cm [24 x 18½ in.]
Paris, Musée d'Orsay

Puvis de Chavannes decided to become a
painter during his first visit to Italy in
1846. Throughout his career he continually
made reference to the Italian tradition,
particularly fresco painting. This picture is
a version of a much larger painting in
which the kinship to mural decoration is
more evident (Paris, Musée d'Orsay, 205 x
154 cm [80¾ x 60⅝ in.]). Although this
composition represents no particular inci-
dent from Greek or Roman mythology,
these women by the seashore are clearly
reminiscent of depictions of Venus and
other classical goddesses. In thus redefin-
ing the classical vocabulary and rendering
figures in a somewhat stylized way, Puvis
de Chavannes formed a crucial bridge
between classicism and modernism.

# CHECKLIST OF WORKS IN THE EXHIBITION

**Jean ALAUX** (called **Le Romain**)
Bordeaux 1785–Paris 1864
*Pensionnaire, 1816–1820*
Director of the Villa Medici, 1847–1852

*François-Édouard Picot in his Studio at the Villa Medici*, 1817 (repr. p. 19)
Oil on canvas, 50.5 x 35.5 cm [19⅞ x 14 in.]
France, Private Collection

**Félix-Joseph BARRIAS**
Paris 1822–Paris 1907
*Pensionnaire, 1845–1849*

*A Gallic Soldier and his Daughter Imprisoned in Rome*, 1847
Oil on canvas, 236 x 171.5 cm [93 x 67½ in.]
Autun, Musée Rolin

**Léon BÉNOUVILLE**
Paris 1821–Paris 1859
*Pensionnaire, 1846–1850*

*The Sculptor Eugène Guillaume*, 1851
Oil on canvas, 47 x 37 cm [18½ x 14½ in.]
Rome, Académie de France

**François-Édouard BERTIN**
Paris 1797–Paris 1871

*View of the Quarries of Cervara, near Rome*, 1839 (repr. p. 36)
Oil on canvas, 180 x 150 cm [70⅞ x 59 in.]
Carcassonne, Musée des Beaux-Arts

**Joseph-Paul BLANC**
Paris 1846–Paris 1904
*Pensionnaire, 1868–1871*

*Perseus*, 1869 (repr. p. 53)
Oil on canvas, 299 x 175 cm [117¾ x 68⅞ in.]
Nîmes, Musée des Beaux-Arts

**Merry-Joseph BLONDEL**
Paris 1781–Paris 1853
*Pensionnaire, 1809–1811*

*The Death of Hyacinth*, 1810 (repr. p. 29)
Oil on canvas, 230 x 151 cm [90½ x 59½ in.]
Gray, Musée Baron Martin

**Guillaume BODINIER**
Paris 1795–Angers 1872

*The Marriage Proposal. Costumes of Albano, near Rome*, 1825 (repr. p. 41)
Oil on canvas, 98 x 135 cm [38½ x 53⅛ in.]

*Seascape*, ca. 1823
Oil on paper, adhered to cardboard, 22 x 30.4 cm [8⅝ x 12 in.]

*Landscape near Rome, The Monte Sacro*, 1823
Oil on paper, adhered to cardboard, 21.9 x 41.5 cm [8⅝ x 16⅜ in.]

*Study of a Rock near the Castel Gandolfo*, 1823
Oil on paper, adhered to cardboard, 22.3 x 30.5 cm [8¾ x 12 in.]

*View of the Roman Campagna, along the Road of Nomentano*, 1823
Oil on paper, adhered to cardboard, 20.3 x 29.4 cm [8 x 11⅝ in.]

*View of the Castle of Ostia*, 1823
Oil on paper, adhered to cardboard, 20.9 x 30.5 cm [8¼ x 12 in.]

*View of Monte Cavo seen from Marino*, 1823
Oil on paper, adhered to cardboard, 20.5 x 30.5 cm [8 x 12 in.]

*Young Bathers on a Rock at Capri*, 1826
Oil on canvas, 28.5 x 42 cm [11¼ x 16½ in.]

*Study of Rocks near Tivoli*, 1823
Oil on paper, adhered to cardboard, 30 x 41.5 cm [11⅞ x 16⅜ in.]

*A Young Boy at the Beach of Terracina*, 1835
Oil on paper, adhered to cardboard, 29.5 x 37.2 cm [11⅝ x 14⅝ in.]

*Copy after a Sketch by Joseph-Désiré Court, the Island of Capri*, 1826
Oil on canvas, adhered to cardboard, 17.5 x 39.5 cm [6⅞ x 15½ in.]

*Waterfall between Rocks*, ca. 1823
Oil on paper, adhered to cardboard, 17.8 x 14.9 cm [7 x 5⅞ in.]

*View of the Lake of Ischia*, 1824
Oil on paper, adhered to cardboard, 17.9 x 41.1 cm [7 x 16⅛ in.]

*View of Saint Peter's in Rome seen from Mount Pincio*, 1824
Oil on paper, adhered to cardboard, 17.8 x 30.4 [7 x 12 in.]

*Pardoned for the Sin of Weakness*, 1825
Oil on paper, adhered to cardboard, 17.7 x 22 cm [7 x 8⅝ in.]

*Panorama of Rome seen from the Gardens of Mount Pincio*, 1824 (repr. p. 35)
Oil on paper, adhered to cardboard, 17.5 x 29.5 cm [6⅞ x 11⅝ in.]

All: Angers, Musée des Beaux-Arts

**Nicolas-Didier BOGUET** the younger (called **Boguet fils**)
Rome 1802–Rome after 1861

*View of the Upper Loggia of the Villa Aldobrandini at Frascati*, ca. 1824
Oil on canvas, 31 x 37.6 cm [12³⁄₁₆ x 14⅞ in.]
Aix-en-Provence, Musée Granet

**Antoine-Félix BOISSELIER**
Paris 1790–Versailles 1857

*View of Lake Nemi*, 1811
Oil on paper adhered to canvas, 32.5 x 48 cm [12¾ x 18⅞ in.]
Washington DC, The Phillips Collection

**Félix BOISSELIER**
Damfal (Haute-Marne) 1776–Rome 1811
*Pensionnaire, 1807–1810*

*A Shepherd Mourning at a Tomb He Erected to a Gnat*, 1808 (repr. p. 28)
Oil on canvas, 195 x 145.5 cm [76¾ x 57¹¹⁄₁₆ in.]
Palm Beach, Mr. and Mrs. Lee Munder

**Léon BONNAT**
Bayonne 1833–Moncy-St.-Éloi 1922

*Interior of the Sistine Chapel*, not dated
Oil on canvas, 45.5 x 50 cm [17⅞ x 19⅝ in.]
Paris, Musée d'Orsay

**Adolphe-William BOUGUEREAU**
La Rochelle 1825–La Rochelle 1905
*Pensionnaire, 1851–1853*

*The Battle between the Centaurs and the Lapiths*, 1852 (repr. p. 52)
Oil on canvas, 123 x 174 cm [48½ x 68½ in.]
Private Collection

*The Engraver Martial Jacques Deveaux*, 1853
Oil on canvas, 47 x 36 cm [18½ x 14³⁄₁₆ in.]

*Self-portrait*, 1854 (repr. p. 16)
Oil on canvas, 47 x 36 cm [18½ x 14³⁄₁₆ in.]
Both: Rome, Académie de France

*Teresa*, ca. 1854
Oil on canvas, 41.9 x 32.2 cm [16½ x 12¹¹⁄₁₆ in.]
Valenciennes, Musée des Beaux-Arts

**Gustave BOULANGER**
Paris 1824–Paris 1888
*Pensionnaire, 1850–1854*

*The Architect Charles Garnier*, 1854
Oil on canvas, 46 x 37 cm [18⅛ x 14⅝ in.]
Rome, Académie de France

**Jean-Louis BRIAN**
Avignon 1805–Paris 1864
*Pensionnaire, 1833–37*

*Joseph-Benoît Suvée*, not dated
Marble, 59 x 29.5 x 26.5 cm [23¼ x 11⅝ x 10⅜ in.]
Rome, Académie de France

**Pierre BRISSET**
1810–1890

*The Engraver Jean-Marie Saint-Ève*, 1846
Oil on canvas, 46 x 37 cm [18⅛ x 14⅝ in.]
Rome, Académie de France

**Alexandre CABANEL**
Montpellier 1823– Paris 1889
*Pensionnaire, 1846–1850*

*Self-portrait at Age 26*, 1849
Oil on canvas, 62 x 54 cm (oval) [24⅜ x 21¼ in.]
Paris, Private Collection

*Study for *The Death of Moses*, ca. 1850 (repr. p. 31)
Graphite, pen and brown ink, gray wash, heightened with gouache on paper, 20 x 27.9 cm [7⅞ x 11 in.]
New York, Dahesh Museum of Art

*The Death of Moses*, 1851 (repr. p. 31)
Oil on canvas, 284.5 x 304.8 cm [112 x 120 in.]
New York, Dahesh Museum of Art

*The Architect Alfred Nicolas Normand*, 1851
Oil on canvas, 46 x 37 cm [18⅛ x 14⅝ in.]

*Self-portrait*, 1851
Oil on canvas, 47 x 37 cm [18½ x 14⅝ in.]
Both: Rome, Académie de France

**Jean-Baptiste CARPEAUX**
Valenciennes 1827–Courbevoie 1875
*Pensionnaire, 1855–1859*

*Nude, after Michelangelo*, not dated
(repr. p. 23)
Oil on canvas, 72.8 x 51.7 cm [28⅝ x 20⅜ in.]

*Two Studies of a Young Woman from Traste-*
*vere*, 1858 (repr. p. 42)
Oil on canvas, 40.3 x 32.5 cm [15⅞ x 12¾ in.]

*Palombella Wearing a 'Panno'*, 1860s
(repr. p. 42)
Terracotta, 68.5 x 50 x 32 cm [27 x 19⅝ x 12⅝ in.]

All: Valenciennes, Musée des Beaux-Arts

**Pierre Jules CAVELIER**
Paris 1814–Paris 1898
*Pensionnaire, 1843–1847*

*The Architect Philippe-Auguste Titeux de*
*Fresnois (1812–1846)*, 1847
Bronze, 36 cm diameter [14⅛ in.]
New York, Charles Janoray Gallery

*Tragedy*, 1854 (repr. p. 55)
Plaster, 86 cm high [33⅞ in.]
New York, Dahesh Museum of Art

**Théodore CHASSÉRIAU**
Santa Domingo 1819–Paris 1856
*A Young Herdsman from the Pontine Marsh-*
*es*, 1841
Oil on canvas, 50 x 44 cm [19⅝ x 17⅜ in.]
Arras, Musée des Beaux-Arts

**François-Nicolas CHIFFLART**
Saint-Omer 1825–Paris 1901
*Pensionnaire, 1852–1856*

*The Villa Medici, Seen from the Garden*,
not dated
Oil on canvas, 26 x 35 cm [10¼ x 13¾ in.]
Valenciennes, Musée des Beaux-Arts

**Léon COGNIET**
Paris 1794–Paris 1880
*Pensionnaire, 1818–1822*

*The Fountain Basin of the Villa Medici in*
*Rome, at Night*, not dated (repr. p. 17)
Oil on paper, adhered to canvas, 20 x 23 cm
[7⅞ x 9 in.]

*Souvenir of Lake Nemi*, not dated
Oil on paper, adhered to canvas, 30.5 x 24.9
cm [12 x 9 ¾ in.]
Both: Orléans, Musée des Beaux-Arts

*The Artist in his Room at the Villa Medici*,
1818 (repr. p. 19)
Oil on canvas, 44.5 x 37 cm [17½ x 14⅝ in.]
Cleveland Museum of Art

*The Sculptor James Pradier*, 1818
Oil on canvas, 47 x 36 cm [18½ x 14⅛ in.]

*The Painter Antoine Thomas*, 1818
Oil on canvas, 47 x 36 cm [18½ x 14⅛ in.]
Both: Rome, Académie de France

**Jules Louis Philippe COIGNET**
Paris 1798–Paris 1860

*A View of Lake Nemi*, 1843
Oil on paper adhered to canvas, 27 x 36 cm
[10⅝ x 14⅛ in.]
Washington DC, National Gallery of Art

**Jean Baptiste Camille COROT**
Paris 1796–Paris 1875

*Rome: View Taken from the Window of the*
*Artist*, 1825 (repr. p. 35)
Oil on paper, adhered to panel, 14.5 x 23.1
cm [5¾ x 9⅛ in.]
Paris, Private Collection

*Rome: Castel Sant'Angelo*, ca. 1826–27,
revised by the artist ca. 1835
Oil on canvas, 34.2 x 46.5 cm [13½ x 18¼ in.]
Williamstown, Sterling and Francine Clark
Art Institute

**Salomon CORRODI**
Fehraltonf (Switzerland) 1810–Como 1892

*View of the Villa Medici and Gardens*,
1844 (repr. p. 16)
Black ink and watercolor on paper,
30 x 45 cm [11 ¾ x 17 ¾ in.]
New York, Didier Aaron, Inc.

**Joseph-Désiré COURT**
Rouen 1797–Rouen 1865
*Pensionnaire, 1822–1826*

*The Composer Victor Rifaut in his Room at*
*the Villa Medici*, 1822
Oil on canvas, 47 x 36 cm [18½ x 14⅛ in.]

*View of the Quarter of Saint John of Lateran*
*in Rome*, ca. 1822
Oil on paper adhered to canvas,
27 x 40.5 cm [10⅝ x 16 in.]

Both: Rouen, Musée des Beaux-Arts

**Pierre-Jean DAVID**, called
**DAVID D'ANGERS**, Angers 1788–Paris 1856
*Pensionnaire, 1812–1815*

*Study for *The Death of Epaminondas, after*
*the Battle of Mantinea*, 1811 (repr. p. 24)
Graphite on paper, 23.8 x 30.6 cm [9⅜ x 12 in.]
New York, Dahesh Museum of Art

*The Death of Epaminondas, after the Battle*
*of Mantinea*, 1811 (repr. p. 24)
Plaster bas-relief, 111.5 x 159 x 22 cm
[43⅞ x 62⅝ x 8⅝ in.]

*Ulysses*, 1814
Marble, 63.5 x 29 x 28.5 cm [25 x 11⅜ x 11¼ in.]

*The Young Herdsman*, or, *Narcissus*, 1816
(repr. p. 25)
Marble, 97 x 46.3 x 43.5 cm [38¼ x 18¼ x 17⅛ in.]
All three: Angers, Galerie David d'Angers

**Jean Baptiste Joseph DEBAY**
Nantes 1802–Paris 1862
*Pensionnaire, 1830–1834*

*Horace Vernet*, 1834 (repr. p. 21)
Marble, 67 x 24.5 x 19.5 cm [26½ x 9⅝ x 7⅝ in.]
Rome, Académie de France

**Edgar Hilaire Germain DEGAS**
Paris 1834–Paris 1917

*Écorché: Right Arm and Shoulder, with the*
*Right Hand Intact*, 1856–58
Charcoal and red chalk on light brown wove
paper, 38 x 26 cm [15 x 10¼ in.]
New York, The Metropolitan Museum of
Art, Gift of Karen B. Cohen

*Study of a Boy Standing with Arms Raised*,
1856
Pencil on pink paper, 28.2 x 21 cm [11⅛ x 8 ¼ in.]
New York, Private Collection

*An Old Italian Woman*, 1857
Oil on canvas, 73.7 x 61 cm [29 x 24]
New York, The Metropolitan Museum of Art

*Dante and Virgil at the Entrance to the*
*Inferno*, 1857–1858 (repr. p. 54)
Oil on canvas, 111.5 x 75.5 cm [44 x 29¾ in.]
Private Collection, courtesy Haggerty Muse-
um of Art, Marquette University, Milwaukee

*Woman on a Terrace*, or *Young Woman and*
*Ibis*, 1857–58, reworked ca. 1860–62 (repr. p. 59)
Oil on canvas, 98 x 74 cm [38⅝ 29⅛ in.]
Private Collection

**Jules-Élie DELAUNAY**
Nantes 1828–Paris 1891
*Pensionnaire from 1857–1860*

**The Communion of the Apostles*, 1861
(repr. p. 47)
Oil on canvas, 280 x 202 cm [110¼ x 79½ in.]
Nantes, Musée des Beaux-Arts

*The Plague in Rome*, 1869 (repr. p. 57)
Oil on canvas, 131 x 176.5 cm [51⅝ x 79½ in.]
Paris, Musée d'Orsay

**Michel-Martin DROLLING**
Paris 1786–Paris 1851
*Pensionnaire, 1811–1815*

*Portrait of Huyot at his Studio in the Villa*
*Medici*, 1812
Oil on canvas, 30 x 39.5 cm [11¾ x 15½ in.]
Paris, École Nationale Supérieure des Beaux-Arts

**Augustin-Alexandre DUMONT**
Paris 1801–Paris 1884
*Pensionnaire, 1824–1828*

*Pierre Narcisse Guérin*, 1829
Marble, 62 x 26 x 20 cm [24⅜ x 10¼ x 7⅞ in.]
Rome, Académie de France

**Louis DUPRÉ**
Versailles 1789–Paris 1837

*Chateaubriand Receiving the Grand-Duchess*
*Helen of Russia in the Garden of the Villa*
*Medici, April 29, 1829* (repr. p. 21)
Oil on canvas, 73 x 97 cm [28¾ x 38¼ in.]
Rome, Académie de France

**Hippolyte FLANDRIN**
Lyon 1809–Rome 1864
*Pensionnaire*, 1833–1837

*The Painter Emile Signol*, 1835
Oil on canvas, 47 x 37 cm [18½ x 14⅝ in.]
Rome, Académie de France

*The Composer Ambroise Thomas*, 1834
Oil on canvas, 64.5 x 54 cm [25⅜ x 21¼ in.]
Montauban, Musée Ingres

*Figure Study: Polites, Son of Priam, Observing the Movements of the Greeks towards Troy*, 1834 (repr. on cover and p. 27)
Oil on canvas, 205 x 148 cm [80¾ x 58¼ in.]
Saint-Étienne, Musée d'Art moderne

Attributed to **Hippolyte Flandrin**
*The Painter Hippolyte Flandrin*, not dated
Oil on canvas, 47 x 36 cm [18½ x 14⅛ in.]
Rome, Académie de France

Attributed to **Hippolyte Flandrin**
*Eve*, not dated
Oil on canvas, 62 x 31 cm [24⅜ x 12¼ in.]
Montauban, Musée Ingres

**Paul FLANDRIN**
Lyon 1811–Paris 1902

**Orangerie of the Villa Borghese*
Oil on paper laid onto canvas, 26.5 x 32 cm [10⅜ x 12⅝ in.]
New York, Didier Aaron, Inc.

*A Herd of Steers in the Roman Campagna*, 1835 (repr. p. 32)
Oil on canvas, 55 x 82 cm [21⅝ x 32¼ in.]
Paris, Private Collection

*An Italian Brigand*, 1835
Oil on cardboard, 32.7 x 22.5 cm [12⅞ x 8⅞ in.]
Paris, Private Collection

*Landscape: The Farewell of an Exile to His Family*, or, *The Sabine Mountains*, 1838 (repr. p. 33)
Oil on canvas, 201 x 150 cm [79⅛ x 59 in.]
Paris, Musée du Louvre

**Denis FOYATIER**
Bussières (Loire) 1793–Paris 1863

*Spartacus*, 1824 (marble version repr. p. 30)
Plaster, 225 x 108 x 71 cm [88½ x 42½ x 28 in.]
Saint-Étienne, Musée d'Art moderne

**Théodore GÉRICAULT**
Rouen 1791–Paris 1824

*The Old Italian Woman*, not dated (repr. p. 40)
Oil on canvas, 62 x 50 cm [24⅜ x 19⅝ in.]
Le Havre, Musée Malraux

**Jean-Léon GÉRÔME**
Vesoul 1824–Paris 1904

*Portrait of a Young Roman Woman*, 1844
Oil on canvas, 59 x 49.5 cm [23¼ x 19½ in.]
Rome, Private Collection

**Félix GIACOMOTTI**
Quingey (Doubs) 1828–Besançon 1909
*Pensionnaire*, 1855–1859

*The Sculptor Jean-Baptiste Carpeaux*, not dated
Oil on canvas, 48 x 38 cm [18⅞ x 15 in.]
Rome, Académie de France

**François-Marius GRANET**
Aix-en-Provence 1775–Aix-en-Provence 1849

*At the Colosseum, A Painter at Work*, not dated (repr. p. 34)
Oil on canvas, 28.5 x 22.5 cm [11¼ x 8⅞ in.]
Private Collection

*View of the Interior of the Colosseum*, 1804 (repr. p. 34)
Oil on canvas, 125 x 160 cm [49¼ x 63 in.]
Paris, Musée du Louvre

***The Crypt of the Basilica di San Martino ai Monti*, ca. 1813
Oil on canvas, 125 x 158 cm [49¼ x 62¼ in.]
Montpellier, Musée Fabre

**The Choir of the Capuchin Church in Rome*, 1815 (repr. p. 37)
Oil on canvas, 196.9 x 148 cm [77½ x 58¼ in.]
New York, The Metropolitan Museum of Art, Gift of L.P. Everard, 1880. (80.5.2). Photograph © 1980 The Metropolitan Museum of Art

**Eugène GUILLAUME**
Montbard (Côte-d'or) 1822–Rome 1905
*Pensionnaire*, 1846–1850
Director of the Villa Medici, 1891–1896

**The Cenotaph of the Gracchi*, 1880 (repr. p. 49)
Marble, 84 x 82 x 40 cm [33 1/16 x 32 5/16 x 15¾ in.]
Cornish, NH, Mr. Max Blumberg and Mr. Carlos Eduardo Araujo

**Hortense HAUDEBOURT-LESCOT**
Paris 1784–Paris 1845

*The Game of the Warm Hand*, 1812
Oil on canvas, 75 x 100 cm [29½ x 39⅜ in.]
Tours, Musée des Beaux-Arts

**Ernest HÉBERT**
Grenoble 1817–La Tronche (Isère) 1908
*Pensionnaire*, 1840–44
Director of the Villa Medici, 1867–1872

***Malaria*, 1848–49 (repr. p. 56)
Oil on canvas, 135 x 193 cm [53⅛ x 76 in.]
Paris, Musée d'Orsay

Attributed to **Ernest Hébert**
*David d'Angers*, not dated (repr. p. 22)
Oil on canvas, 55 x 46 cm [21¾ x 18⅛ in.]

Attributed to **Ernest Hébert**
*Jean Auguste Dominique Ingres*, not dated (repr. p. 22)
Oil on canvas, 46 x 38 cm [18⅛ x 15 in.]

Both: Rome, Académie de France

**Ernest HIOLLE**
Paris 1834–Bois-le-Roi 1886
*Pensionnaire*, 1863–1867

*Narcissus*, 1868 (repr. p. 50)
Marble, 87 x 160 x 64 cm [34¼ x 63 x 25¼ in.]
*The Painter Joseph-Fortunet Layraud*, 1868
Bronze, 55.2 x 23 x 25.5 cm [21¾ x 9 x 10 in.]

Both: Valenciennes, Musée des Beaux-Arts

**Jean Auguste Dominique INGRES**
Montauban 1780–Paris 1867
*Pensionnaire*, 1805–1810
Director of the Villa Medici, 1835–1840

*Male Torso*, 1800 (repr. p. 23)
Oil on canvas, 100 x 80 cm [39¼ x 31½ in.]

*The Ambassadors of Agamemnon in the Tent of Achilles*, 1801 (repr. p. 25)
Oil on canvas, 113 x 146 cm [44½ x 57½ in.]

Both: Paris, École Nationale Supérieure des Beaux-Arts

*Study of an Old Man*, ca. 1800
Oil on canvas, 70 x 55 cm [27½ x 21¾ in.]
Aix-en-Provence, Musée Granet

*François-Marius Granet*, 1807–1809 (repr. p. 18)
Oil on canvas, 74.5 x 63.2 cm [29⅜ x 24⅞ in.]
Aix-en-Provence, Musée Granet

*Pope Pius VII in the Sistine Chapel*, 1814 (repr. p. 37)
Oil on canvas, 74.5 x 92.7 cm [29⅜ x 36½ in.]
Washington DC, National Gallery of Art

**INGRES and Studio,** probably
**Jean-François MONTESSUY** (1804–1876)
Recent attribution by Georges Vigne

**Oedipus and the Sphinx*, not dated
Oil on canvas, 165 x 103 cm [65 x 40½ in.]
Angers, Musée des Beaux-Arts

**Jean Louis Nicolas JALEY**
Paris 1802–Neuilly-sur-Seine 1866
*Pensionnaire*, 1828–1832

*Modesty*, 1833 (repr. p. 45)
Marble, 116 x 47 x 37 cm [45⅝ x 18½ x 14 ⅝ in.]
Paris, Musée du Louvre

**Jules LAFRANCE**
Paris 1841–Paris 1881
*Pensionnaire*, 1871–1874

*The Infant Saint John the Baptist*, ca. 1878
Marble, 149 x 62 x 64 cm [58⅝ x 24⅜ x 25¼ in.]
Paris, Musée d'Orsay

**Charles-Philippe LARIVIÈRE**
Paris 1798– Paris 1876
*Pensionnaire*, 1825–1829

*View of the Gardens of the Villa Medici*, not dated
Oil on canvas, 32.3 x 53 cm [12 ¾ x 20⅞ in.]

*A Roman Villa*, not dated
Oil on cardboard, 24.9 x 21.8 cm [9 ¾ x 8 ⅝ in.]

*The Arch of Septimus Severus*, ca. 1825
Oil on paper, adhered to canvas, 24.5 x 31.5 cm [9⅝ x 12⅜ in.]

*The Arch of Constantine, seen from an Arcade of the Coliseum*, 1827
Oil on canvas, 44.6 x 33.9 cm [17½ x 13⅜ in.]

*The Forum at Pompeii*, 1830
Oil on panel, 23.2 x 30.2 cm [9⅛ x 11⅞ in.]

All: Amiens, Musée de Picardie

**Henri LEHMANN**
Kiel (Germany) 1814–Paris 1882

*Study for *Saint Catherine of Alexandria Carried to Her Tomb*, ca. 1839 (repr. p. 46)
Graphite on paper, 50.8 x 88.8 cm [20 x 35 in.]
New York, Dahesh Museum of Art, Gift of DeCourcy E. McIntosh

*Saint Catherine of Alexandria Carried to Her Tomb*, 1839 (repr. p. 46)
Oil on canvas, 152 x 262 cm [59⅞ x 103⅛ in.]
Montpellier, Musée Fabre

**Louis-Hector LEROUX**
Verdun 1829–Angers 1900

***A Funeral in the Columbarium of the Casa dei Cesari at Porta Capena in Rome*, 1864
Oil on canvas, 141.5 x 101.5 cm [55¾ x 40 in.]
Paris, Musée d'Orsay

**Jules LENEPVEU**
Angers 1819–Paris 1898
*Pensionnaire*, 1848–1852
Director of the Villa Medici, 1872–1878

**Study of an Italian Model* (repr. p. 41)
Oil on canvas, 50 x37 cm [19¹¹⁄₁₆ x 14⁹⁄₁₆ in.]
Maine, Private Collection

**Emile LÉVY**
Paris 1826–Paris 1890
*Pensionnaire*, 1855–1857

*Ruth and Noemi*, ca 1856
Oil on canvas, 151 x 112 cm [59½ x 44⅛ in.]
Rouen, Musée des Beaux-Arts

**René-Ambroise MARÉCHAL**
Paris 1818–Rome 1847
*Pensionnaire*, 1844–1847

***ROMA (Allegory of Modern Rome)*, 1847
Marble, 78 x 41 x 40 cm [30¾ x 16⅛ x 15¾ in.]
Paris, Musée du Louvre

**Luc-Olivier MERSON**
Paris 1846–Paris 1920
*Pensionnaire*, 1870–1873

*Saint-Edmond, King of England, Martyr*, 1871 (repr. p. 51)
Oil on canvas, 145.5 x 226 cm [57¼ x 89 in.]
Troyes, Musée des Beaux-Arts

**Achille-Etna MICHALLON**
Paris 1796–Paris 1822
*Pensionnaire*, 1818–1821

*Mazzochi, an Italian Brigand*, not dated (repr. p. 38)
Oil on canvas, 35 x 27 cm [13¾ x 10⅝ in.]

*View of the Villa Medici through an Arch*, ca. 1818 (repr. p. 17)
Oil on paper, adhered to canvas, 22 x 29.5 cm [8⅝ x 11⅝ in.]

Both: Orléans, Musée des Beaux-Arts

**Gustave MOREAU**
Paris 1826–Paris 1898

*Hesiod and the Muses*, ca. 1860 (repr. p. 58)
Oil on canvas, 133 x 133 cm [52⅜ x 52⅜ in.]
Paris, Musée Gustave Moreau

**François-Joseph NAVEZ**
Charleroi 1787–Brussels 1869

*Musical Scene, People from Trastevere*, 1821
Oil on canvas, 116 x 138 cm [45⅝ x 54¾ in.]
Williamstown, Sterling & Francine Clark Art Institute

**Edme-Antony-Paul NOËL**, called **Tony-Noël**
Paris 1845–Palaiseau 1909
*Pensionnaire*, 1869–1872

*Ernest Hébert*, 1872
Bronze, 67 x 39 x 30 cm [26⅜ x 15⅜ x 11¾ in.]
Rome, Académie de France

**Auguste OTTIN**
Paris 1811–Paris 1890
*Pensionnaire*, 1837–1840

*Jean Auguste Dominique Ingres*, 1840
Marble, 61 x 28 x 23 cm [24 x 11 x 9 in.]
Rome, Académie de France

**Dominique PAPETY**
Marseille 1815–Marseille 1849
*Pensionnaire*, 1837–1841

*Praying to the Madonna*, not dated
Oil on panel, 38 x 46 cm [15 x 18⅛ in.]
Nantes, Musée des Beaux-Arts

**Jean Joseph PERRAUD**
Monay 1819–Paris 1876
*Pensionnaire*, 1848–1852

*The Farewell of Jason*, 1848–49 (repr. p. 48)
Plaster bas-relief, 197 x 182 x 24.5 cm [77½ x 71⅝ x 9⅝ in.]
Lons-le-Saunier, Musée des Beaux-Arts

*Jean Alaux*, 1853
Marble, 68 x 51 x 34 cm [26¾ x 20⅛ x 13⅜ in.]
Rome, Académie de France

**Louis-Messidor-Lebon PETITOT**
Paris 1794–Paris 1862
*Pensionnaire*, 1815–1819

*A Young Hunter Wounded by a Serpent*, 1825–1827 (repr. p. 26)
Marble, 136 x 95.1 x 50.1 cm [53½ x 37½ x 19¾ in.]
Paris, Musée du Louvre

**Pierre PUVIS DE CHAVANNES**
Lyon 1824–Paris 1898

*Young Women at the Seashore*, 1881 (repr. p. 60)
Oil on canvas, 61 x 47 cm [24 x 18½ in.]
Paris, Musée d'Orsay

**Jean-Victor SCHNETZ**
Versailles 1787–Paris 1870
Director of the Villa Medici, 1841–1846 and 1853–1865

*The Fortune-teller*, not dated (repr. p. 40)
Oil on canvas, 74.5 x 62.3 cm [29⅜ x 24½ in.]
Clermont-Ferrand, Musée d'art Roger-Quillot

**François-Charles SELLIER**
1830–1882
*Pensionnaire*, 1858–1862

*The Composer Georges Bizet*, not dated
Oil on canvas, 47 x 37 cm [18½ x 14⅝ in.]
Rome, Académie de France

*Italian Woman*, ca. 1860
Oil on canvas, 103 x 76.7 cm [40½ x 30¼ in.]
Paris, Musée d'Orsay

**Émile Jean Horace VERNET**
Paris 1789–Paris 1863
Director of the Villa Medici, 1829–1834

**The Start of the Race of Riderless Horses*, ca. 1820 (repr. p. 43)
Oil on canvas, 46 x 54 cm [18⅛ x 21¼ in.]
New York, The Metropolitan Museum of Art, Catharine Lorillard Wolfe Collection, Bequest of Catharine Lorillard Wolfe, 1887. (87.15.47). Photograph © 1994 The Metropolitan Museum of Art

*Italian Brigands Surprised by the Papal Troops*, 1830
Oil on canvas, 86.3 x 131.5 cm [34 x 51¾ in.]
Baltimore, The Walters Art Museum

*The Confession of a Brigand*, 1831 (repr. p. 39)
Oil on canvas, 150 x 230 cm [59 x 90½ in.]
Paris, Private Collection

*Portrait of the Artist in his Studio*, 1832 (repr. p. 20)
Oil on canvas, 65 x 54.2 cm [25⅝ x 21⅜ in.]
Cleveland Museum of Art

*Louise Vernet*, not dated (repr. p. 20)
Oil on canvas, 100 x 74 cm [39⅜ x 29⅛ in.]
Paris, Musée du Louvre

**Unknown Artist**

*The Engraver André-Benoist Barreau, called Taurel*, ca. 1818
Oil on canvas, 47 x 37 cm [18½ x 14⅝ in.]
Rome, Académie de France

**Unknown Artist**

*The Painter Paul Baudry*, not dated
Oil on canvas, 47 x 37 cm [18⅛ x 14⅝ in.]
Rome, Académie de France

**Unknown Artist**

*The Painter Fortuné Layraud*, not dated
Oil on canvas, 46 x 37 cm [18⅛ x 14⅝ in.]
Rome, Académie de France

**Unknown Artist**

*The Painter Édouard Toudouze*, not dated
Oil on canvas, 46 x 35 cm [18⅛ x 13¾ in.]
Rome, Académie de France

**Unknown Artist**

*The Painter Dominique Papety*, not dated
Oil on canvas, 47 x 38 cm [18⅛ x 15 in.]
Rome, Académie de France

* EXHIBITED IN NEW YORK ONLY

** EXHIBITED IN ROME AT THE SCUDERIE DEL QUIRINALE (SEE PAGE 5 NOTE 1)